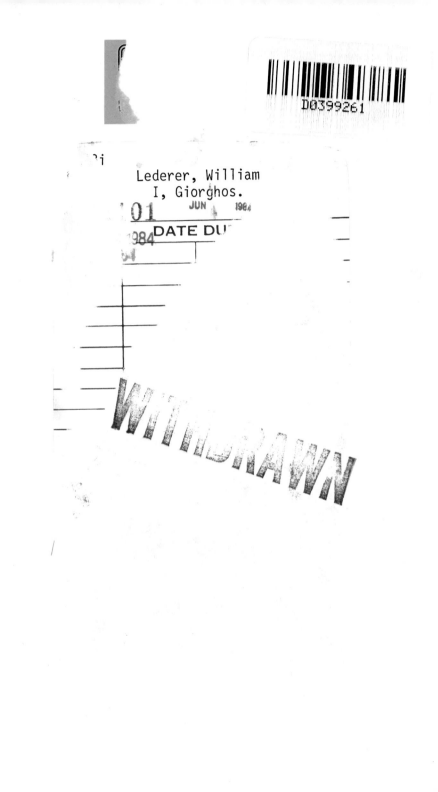

I, GIORGHOS

W · W · NORTON & COMPANY

NEW YORK · LONDON

I, GIORGHOS

A NOVEL

WILLIAM J. LEDERER

The text of this book is composed in Janson, with display type set in Augustea Inline.
Composition and Manufacturing by The Haddon Craftsmen, Inc. Book design by
Antonina Krass.

First Edition

Library of Congress Cataloging in Publication Data
Lederer, William J., 1912–
I, Giorghos.
I. Title
PS3562.E312 1984   813'.54   83–42670

ISBN 0-393-01788-5

W· W· Norton & Company, Inc., 500 Fifth Avenue, New York, N. Y. 10110
W· W· Norton & Company Ltd., 37 Great Russell Street, London WC1B 3NU
1 2 3 4 5 6 7 8 9 0

PREFACE

Even though George Adamson is a native-born American, for six months he wrote his diaries in Greek. As his publisher and translator, I have tried to keep the English version of *I, Giorghos* congruous with the original. I have kept punctuation, word rhythms, sentence structure, and dialogue patterns consonant with the way George wrote the material in Greek. Sometimes I spelled his name Giorghos and sometimes Giorgho, as is proper in the Greek language. There are a few words I did not anglicize, for example, *caris*. The English translation, *charis*, does not have the same meaning. At one point I put in a long letter that George had written me. The letter supplied information lacking in the journals.

It was important to me that my translation mirrored everything that George had felt, sensed, and written about. I wanted American readers to experience the same excitement, joy, and uplift that I had experienced when I first read George's account of his adventure.

Agios Papandillis
Zeuss Publishing Company
Athens, Greece

I,
GIORGHOS

STARTING MY DIARY AGAIN
SUNDAY, 16 APRIL 1967
BROOKLYN, N.Y.

I finally forced myself to call Agios. I placed the call last Thursday. It was 8:00 A.M. in Athens and almost midnight here. Agios himself answered the phone. I said, "Agios, this is George Adamson. . . ." I'm calling from New York. . . ."

"Giorgho, old friend, how are you?"

"I need help."

"Oh?"

I told him that for some months everything in my life had been threatened. First, I needed a lot of money.

He said, "Write the saints book for me. You should have done it long ago." Without hesitation, he agreed to the $10,000 advance I needed. I started to tell him what else I needed, but he interrupted, "The timing is perfect for the saints. We'll have to hurry. Listen, Giorgho, come to Athens on the flight that leaves New York on Sunday night. A few other friends of mine will be on the same plane. I'll meet you in Athens on Monday morning. We'll turn the world upside down the same as we did eleven years ago."

That was Thursday. Today is Sunday. All afternoon, even though I was badly hung over and tired, I rushed around and thoroughly cleaned my house. If I am to die soon, I want people to find my place clean.

The plane ticket is in my pocket. My luggage, typewriter, and old gray canvas knapsack are by the front door. The taxi has been ordered.

6:15 P.M. — WAITING TO BOARD PLANE
SUNDAY, 16 APRIL 1967
JFK INTERNATIONAL AIRPORT

~~~~~~~~~~~~~~~~~~~~~~~~~

The taxi got tied up in traffic; and I was afraid I'd miss the plane. When I got to the airport, there were no porters available. There never are any porters if one is exhausted, late, and has tons of luggage. I picked up my tons of luggage and staggered along what seemed an endless distance to the ticket counter. I had to stop every few minutes to rest.

Out of breath and perspiring, I finally got to the counter. While the ticket clerk was processing my ticket and luggage, I couldn't stop ogling her breasts, neck, and long yellow hair; and I had my usual fantasies. She stamped my papers, handed them back to me, and said, "Mister Adamson, I've put the senior citizen blue card on your ticket. Special treatment for older passengers. You can board about ten minutes before the others. Have a good flight, sir."

God, do I look that old?

The flight is scheduled to depart at 7 P.M. and arrive in Athens at 10 A.M. Monday, 17 April — my fifty-seventh birthday.

13

SUNDAY, 16 APRIL 1967
ON BOARD OLYMPIC AIRWAYS PLANE,
WAITING FOR TAKE-OFF, N.Y. TO ATHENS

I'm the only one in the plane so far. When I began to fasten my seat belt, I had to lengthen it considerably. I'm forty pounds heavier than I was the last time I flew to Greece. That trip was one of joyful ebullience. Now I'm sweating blood. I owe money all over the place, including a $5,000 payment on Sheila's divorce settlement. Thank God for the advance I'll get from Agios. But I have to write a book for it. Hell, I don't even know if I can I write the book! I haven't had a success since my last trip to Greece — and since marrying Sheila. I'm not blaming her entirely. Perhaps getting old and being in bad health has slowed me down?

My birthday starts at midnight. Will my birthday be like Papa's fifty-seventh? He died of a heart attack two days later. I'm worrying about *my* recent heart attack. God, I must be in worse health than I thought. That ticket clerk taking me to be a senior citizen!

Perhaps what depresses me most right now is the thought of traveling with a planeload of strangers on this particular eight-hour flight. It seems terrible — frightening — to be without friends or family on one's birthday evening. I wonder if any of Agios' friends will be in first class?

In a few minutes the "younger" passengers will embark. I'll try to sleep. I'm utterly exhausted.

16–17 APRIL 1967

IN FLIGHT, N.Y. TO ATHENS

~~~~~~

S omeone — the woman next to me — touched my shoulder, and said in Greek, "Mister Adamson, do you want to wake up for cocktails and dinner?" I rubbed my eyes and grunted. The woman said, "Happy birthday, Giorgho Adamson!" I looked at her and when my eyes focused I thought perhaps I already was dead. Dear God — it was Ilya, whom I'd lost fifty-one years ago! Yes, Ilya — her black braids hanging over her red woolen cape, the unmistakable round Greek face, the clear olive-colored skin, her warm dimpled smile.

Ilya asked me if I was ill. Was anything wrong? Then I knew it was not Ilya. This woman's voice was different; and she was older and a bit heavier.

I told her I had been startled because she resembled my childhood Greek nurse — who practically had been my mother. The woman laughed (Ilya's understanding and approving laugh); and then I asked her how she had known my name and also how had she known that in a few hours it would be my birthday?

We were talking in Greek. I hadn't spoken in Greek in eleven years.

"Agios called and said you'd be on this flight."

She handed me a day-old Greek newspaper. A front-page story on me started off with "Giorghos Adamson, famous author of *Mount Athos, the Holy Mountain,* is coming 'home' to write a book about the greatest Greek saints." There was a picture of me taken in Athens the last time I was there. I looked like a young man. I was lean, alive, bursting with confidence.

The woman introduced herself, Maria Papadopoulou from the island of Lesvos. She's an old friend of Agios'. Of course almost everyone in Greece is an old friend of Agios'. And then she showed me the paragraph about a press conference that Agios had planned for me at the airport.

She looked at her watch and clapped her hands, "It's past midnight in Athens — so it's already your birthday in Greece. Happy birthday!" she shouted, waving her arms, exuding Greek energy and enthusiasm.

The people around us were Greeks. They reached over, shook my hand, slapped my back, and began calling for drinks. I began enjoying myself, and even made a short, loud speech about how wonderful it was to be going home again.

We drank and toasted before dinner, through dinner and after dinner. It was the best birthday party I'd had in years. Gradually the others quieted down and went to sleep; but Maria and I kept on drinking, talking, and laughing as if we had known each other and each other's family for years.

Then I had one drink too many, and for a while I again imagined that the woman sitting next to me was my old nurse Ilya. My hidden emotions poured out. I began babbling how I hated Mimi, Papa's third wife, and how I hated Papa. I hated them because they had discharged Ilya and had dumped me into a foster home so that they could travel.

I paused and breathed deeply in the effort to stop more upheavals from clawing their way up from my guts. I resisted talking. I clamped my mouth shut — so hard that my cheek muscles hurt. It was of no use. The words poured out. I guess I was shouting because Maria said, "Shhh, not so loud, you'll wake up the others."

Nevertheless I continued. Leaning forward, my face only a few inches from Maria's — to make certain she heard me — I told her that my stepmother and Sheila resembled each other so closely they could be sisters. And further, I confessed that the many women with whom I had had affairs over the last forty years — every one of them also had resembled Mimi. But Sheila was most like her, the same build, the same mannerisms, the same voice, the same behavior patterns. In great detail I described Sheila's beauty and sensuality; and how I had become obsessed with an almost uncontrollable physical passion for her.

Maria stopped me by placing her hand over my mouth. When she was satisfied that I had quieted down, she spoke softly: "Ah, Giorgho, your life's like an ancient Greek tragedy — you marrying the beautiful daughter or twin of the beautiful stepmother you hated." She lowered her hand from my mouth, placed it over her own, yawned, and said, "We both should get some sleep. But first," she added, "I'm going to the toilet."

I watched her walk up the aisle — Maria Papadopoulou, a middle-aged, chunky Greek woman with superb muscles, tight buttocks, and a flexible waist. Compared to Sheila, she appeared old and fat. But from the way she moved, she looked like the type who enjoyed sex and was wise from many affairs.

She returned and immediately went to sleep. I drank what was left in my glass and in Maria's glass; and then, unsteadily and holding on to the seats for support, went to the washroom. I shaved. I did this very slowly and carefully because I had slight tremors from too much booze and too much excitement. I changed my shirt and groomed myself. I wanted to get off the plane looking neat — especially since I was scheduled to meet the press.

MONDAY, 17 APRIL 1967
ATHENS

~~~~~~~~~~~~~~~~~

Agios met me at the ramp. Short, broad-shouldered, power-ful, big white teeth, his gray hair accentuating his dark skin. His nickname as a general of the guerrillas had been "Hercules."

We embraced, touching cheeks — then he stepped back, looking at me as if I were a ghost. He stared, then in his deep rasping voice asked me what was the matter? Had I been ill?

Maria came down the ramp and stood next to me. "Agios," I said, "Maria and I . . ." He embraced her briefly, but he continued to stare at me, frowning. He brusquely pulled me a few feet back, making room to let the other passengers off; and then, turning to the man standing next to him, he spoke in the man's ear. The man nodded and hurried off to the terminal building.

Agios put his arm around me and said he didn't want me to meet the press now. He had just canceled the press conference. The report-ers, he said, still remembered me as I had been eleven years ago after mountain climbing all over Greece. "Giorgho," he said, "they wrote of you as shining with what they called 'the Greek Radiance.' They compared you with the virile Hemingway, the incandescent Kazantzakis, the earthshaking Homer. Those write-ups made the book a success. They started my fortune as a publisher."

I tried to interrupt him to say I could put on a good show. He pushed me still farther away from the disembarking passengers and continued, authoritatively and gruffly, telling me that Greek journalists know little about art or literature. They write about their impressions of the author. If the author's a heroic figure, the book gets good publicity. If the author looks like a weakling or a weasel, they ignore him. Agios paused and smiled, but it was a smile of power-in-action. It was not the warm, joyful smile of an old friend.

He scolded, telling me that because I was in anarchy (oh, the Greek word is so subtle and precise!) he had stalled off the press conference until I was in charge of myself again — in charge and presentable. Then, as if he were describing an enemy, he went into details — to prove the validity of his decision. "Giorgho, my God, your face is pasty — like a death mask. You smell of fear and look like a whipped slave. You look as if Saint Gregory's demons have been eating you."

It was true. I had been in magnificent shape at the last press conference in Athens. Also I had had the certitude of an author who has several books on the best-seller list. It was then I was having an affair with Sheila. We weren't married yet. I was forty-six and making love to a gorgeous thirty-year-old woman who was sought after by almost every male in town. That she still was married to John made no difference.

Agios continued, "Giorgho, my old, dear friend and colleague, we shouldn't even discuss the book until you've had a vacation and have recuperated. God, you look terrible. Now let's see . . . where can I hide you for a couple of weeks?"

Maria stepped between us. She looked at Agios, acknowledging that he was in command. "Agios," she said, "I have a villa. . . ."

Suddenly Agios smiled broadly and hugged her, "Ah, Maria, you're a godsend. For at least a week, two weeks — good! good!"

He discussed the situation with Maria — as if I weren't present and as if I had no say in the matter. He spoke like a general who is winning a campaign again. He said that his assistant would tell the press I was ill — I'd had an accident — his assistant would make up the details so that the press would have some sort of a story — that I'd be at a private nursing home for a week or two. The plan was to get me to Lesvos as soon as possible. "There's an early afternoon plane. Here, get into my car [which he had on the field]. We'll lunch at Passalimani and talk about your advance — and then to the airport." I asked what about my luggage and Immigration. He said he'd already taken care of everything — and pushed me into his limousine.

We drove out through the "For Employees Only" gate. The security guards saluted General Hercules.

In Agios' car on the way to Passalimani, Maria took my hand for a moment, and smiled. Agios enthusiastically reminded me what a great success my last book on Greece had been. He chattered away that *Mount Athos, the Holy Mountain* was in every school, in every church wherever there were Greeks in the world, that it was in almost every Greek home. He said that it took an author with deep spirituality, a sense of history, a great reporter's eye to produce such a book. "And, by God," he said, "I have a hunch this one will be even better."

He spoke to me as if he were General Hercules persuading a frightened soldier to collect himself and be brave. It's okay. I thought, for the goddam general safe at headquarters to give a rah-rah speech. It's not his ass that's about to be shot away. Hell, mine's already filled with shrapnel.

I recalled that when the plane was landing in Athens I had had a spurt of optimism, a hope that once I was in Greece everything would turn around. I had expected that Agios' warm welcome and the enthusiasm at the press conference would give me back my old confidence. Instead, that was when my ass got filled with shrapnel.

The car stopped. Agios said, "We're here. A good lunch will pep you up, Giorgho. This place has the best seafood in Greece."

The thought of fish made my stomach flutter. But the first glass of ouzo settled me down. The sight of Passalimani harbor quickened me. Who can resist the splendor of the blue Aegean reflecting the sunshine of Hellas? I felt that I was pulling out of my funk. But very slowly. The incident at the airport had dulled my senses. People and events had moved about me like gray blurs. However during lunch my senses gradually began focusing again. I heard Greeks shouting. I felt the ocean breeze. I smelled the sea and the herb-filled Greek food. I saw the taxis rushing along the beachside highway. I saw the boats in the harbor, and I tried to read their names and the hailports that told where they came from. I breathed deeply, and there was no ache anymore.

During the last part of the meal, Agios brought up the subject of the new book. I heard the sound and intonations of his voice, but not the actual words he was saying. My mind was out in the Aegean. Whenever Agios paused, I automatically nodded in agreement. Maria made comments from time to time, and I nodded then too.

I wasn't focusing on the conversation because I was fascinated by an ancient red boat moored about a hundred yards away. She obviously was Hellenic, broad of beam, constructed from stout, hand-hewn timbers. And she was old. Her broken rail, her rusted exhaust pipe, her frayed lines, told that the boat needed work. But despite her shabbiness, she had the look of indestructibility and well-earned arrogance. And she was dressed for the part — painted bloodred all over. Even the mast. On her bow were painted two huge blue-and-white eyes. They were oval and each about two feet across.

Agios coughed, placed his hand on my wrist. "Well," he said, "then it's agreed. We'll draw up the contract while you're in Lesvos. The advance is satisfactory?"

I nodded.

I turned to the boat again. Something about her gaudy complexion gave her life; and her thick timbers, battered here, bruised there, seemed to suggest that as a couple of old warriors we should get to know each other.

From beyond the red boat, the wind carried the odor of distant shores — of spices, wineshops, graveyards, perspiring olive pickers, and stonemasons. The swaying boom made rumbling bass sounds punctuated by a few high-pitched notes as it chafed against the mast. It was the song of Greek stevedores and seamen.

Agios broke into my fantasy to say that he had ordered a limousine to take Maria and me to the airport. Then he chuckled and told me that the red boat I was staring at was a very old and famous boat that had carried ammunition to Crete during the rebellion.

Ten minutes later, Maria and I waited by the seawall for the limousine. The red boat was about thirty yards away, creaking and muttering as she thrust up and down on the Mediterranean swells. The waves probably were her old friends from blood-soaked Cyprus, from Lesvos, from Crete; or maybe from crowded Mers-el-Kebir or even flinty Gibralter.

A large, crudely painted sign in both Greek and English hung off her side: FOR SALE, CHEAP. The blue eyes on the bow looked directly at me. Four thousand years ago, Odysseus' boat had eyes like that on her bow. It is said that they navigated while Odysseus slept.

Topside, a tanned, wiry man wearing a captain's black cap hurried forward when he saw me. He was barefoot and shirtless. His dungaree trousers were held up by an old piece of line wrapped around his waist. Raising his arms, he said loudly in English, "You want to buy her? I'll give you a good bargain."

The limousine arrived.

The man on the boat shouted that I could have her for a hundred thousand drachmas, that it was the buy of a lifetime, and that he had to sell. As our car moved off, I smiled at him and he shouted, "Wait! Wait!" I turned my head and again saw the boat's broken rails, her frayed halyards. But most of all I saw the blue-and-white eyes staring at me from within their bloodred skull.

Three thousand dollars for an old Greek sailboat? I wondered why it was so cheap. Probably a swindle, like the selling of the Brooklyn Bridge. Why should I buy a boat anyway? There was no reason. Further, I knew little about sailboats or sailing. I hadn't sailed since I was fifteen, and even before that I had not done much of it. In the navy, my only seagoing experience had been in destroyers. But the boat tugged at my insides. From the first moment I had seen her, I had felt a sense of intimacy with that old red warrior.

MONDAY, 17 APRIL 1967

LESVOS

~~~~~~~~~~~~~~~~~~~~~~~~~

When we arrived here about an hour ago, 5 P.M., I was numb with fatigue. The jet lag and the hectic activities of the last two days had drained me. Maria's villa is near the village of Mythymna, about three-quarters of an hour from the airport. In front of the house, a beach of white sand leads into startlingly blue water. Groves of gnarled olive trees surround the estate, and sheep graze in the pasture. There is a garden of fruit trees and vegetables.

I told Maria that despite my extreme weariness, I already could feel the vitality of the place. She nodded and said that 2,400 years ago Hippocrates had sent his convalescing patients here. "The Temple of Healing is about half an hour's walk from here, close by Uncle Andrew's clinic. That's why he chose the location — because of its natural healing energies."

"Uncle Andrew?"

"The doctor who'll examine you. Oh, excuse me, Giorgho, I must telephone him and make an appointment."

She left the room. I thought about getting the luggage from the car, but instead I sprawled in a chair, my eyes heavy, my bones aching; and I fell asleep. When Maria shook me, I vaguely heard her say that we were to be at the doctor's office at seven tomorrow morning; and I was not to eat anything until after the examination. She helped me out of the chair and led me into my bedroom.

TUESDAY, 18 APRIL 1967

LESVOS

~~~~~~~~~~~~~~~~~~

E ven after twelve hours of sleep, I still found it difficult to get up this morning. The jet lag still disrupted me. I felt impatient and irritable. On the way to the doctor's office, I asked Maria many questions. I learned that it was Agios who had suggested a physical examination. The doctor, Maria's uncle, was a priest as well as a physician — Bishop Andrew Simonoptritus. Maria said he was very old, very wise, and famous as a healer.

He walked down the path to meet us, his white beard swaying over his chest and his arms outstretched in welcome. The moment I saw him I felt better. He moved with ease, looking almost as if he were a ballet dancer playing the part of an elderly bishop. Everything about him appeared relaxed and in balance. Yet I felt there was nothing random about his movements or behavior. I had the impression that he smiled warmly because he was glad to see us. The way he placed his feet, the way he held his back straight and his head high, his ancient, healthy-looking leanness, none of these was random. I *knew* they were the result of conscious training — a consciousness that allowed true spontaneity, actions and thoughts coming from free will, not blind habit. Just by looking at him, I felt stimulated and quickened. The air of the man was the one that I always had wanted for myself. Occasionally I'd approached it when I was alone, climbing mountains, or in moments of great hazard. But such times were rare, and here, now, I was at the other end of the pole.

Once we were in his office, the bishop-doctor immediately went to work on me. He asked no questions. For about an hour he didn't say a word. Here was a physician who was personally observing before being influenced by the patient's subjective description. He used his stethoscope all over me, even on my extremities. He thumped me and listened. He tested my muscle tone. He looked at my ears, eyes, rectum, genitals, hands, feet — he observed every square inch of me. I felt that here was an experienced professional who cared about his patients. He hooked me up to an electrocardiograph, had me run in place until I was exhausted, then rest, then continue running.

I asked him, "How is it that you, a bishop, are also a physician?"

"Long ago," he said, taking the stethoscope from his ears for a few moments, "I felt that the body, the mind, and the spirit each are separate entities and yet, still, they are one — just like the Holy Trinity. Each is equally sacred and each requires equal attention. If one of them gets polluted or sick, then the others also malfunction; and as we're made in the image of God, every part of us must be as healthy as possible or we are an insult to God. So I decided that if I were to be a priest, I would have to know as much about the body and mind as I knew about the spirit. I studied the body at medical school. . . ."

"Heidelberg," said Maria, smiling proudly.

"I studied the mind with a psychiatrist."

"Doctor Carl Jung," said Maria.

I said, "What have you found wrong with me?"

The bishop-doctor coughed, held up his hand the way a policeman does to halt traffic, and then said, "Maria told me there's a history of coronary problems in your family — that your father died of a heart attack."

"Yes, that's so," I said.

"How old was he?"

"Fifty-seven — the same age as I am."

"Have you had any symptoms of heart problems?"

"I had an attack about six months ago."

"Tell me about it. Tell me everything you can remember. Tell me everything that happened before and after the attack."

I said, "It happened about six at night. I was walking home and suddenly I felt . . ."

He interrupted and very gently said, "Giorgho, what happened earlier? Had anything exciting happened the day before?"

"Sheila and I had had a hell of a fight."

"What about?"

"She'd ordered a color television for the girls' room. We'd argued about this previously, and I'd forbidden her to buy the TV because there already were three television sets in the house and because I didn't have the money.

"Then during lunch that day, the TV store delivered the set to the house. I sent it back. That's what started the fight."

"How long did it last?"

"All afternoon, until about seven at night. Sheila then put on her sexiest-looking dress and said she was going to a party where she would find someone who'd appreciate her. And she left."

"What did you do?"

"I stayed home and got drunk."

"What time did you get up the next morning, the day of your attack?"

"About eight o'clock."

"What's the first thing you recall happening that day?"

"I got a special delivery letter from Mimi — my stepmother — forwarding a bill for nine hundred dollars from the cemetery for the upkeep of my father's grave. It threw me into a rage. Why should

I pay for the bastard's grave. He never did anything for me except let Mimi put me into an orphanage. I told Sheila about the bill because I wanted confirmation that it was an outrage. Instead, she told me I was the cheapest son of a bitch she'd ever known — and the most stupid. Then she returned to the subject of the television set. She shouted that the set had been all paid for before it had been delivered and that she had paid for it with her own money. I asked her why hadn't she told me that yesterday. She said I hadn't given her a chance, what with my tantrums and screaming when the set was delivered. At that point we got into another terrible fight."

"Then what?"

"I left the house and went to the club. I had a heck of a big lunch and a barrel of martinis."

"Then what?"

"I started home. I wondered if perhaps I oughtn't to go elsewhere instead of returning home and fighting a battle I was certain to lose; and then I remembered that this was the afternoon that Sheila had her blasted psychology group at the house; and I thought it might be amusing to go back and heckle them and make a pest of myself. It was drizzling and it was hard to find a cab, so I walked to Fifth Avenue. I saw Saint Patrick's, where Ilya — my nurse when I was a child — had frequently taken me when things got hectic at home . . ."

"Saint Patrick's?"

"Saint Patrick's Cathedral. I saw it and decided to go there and try to find some peace and perhaps try to pray the way Ilya had taught me — even though I didn't understand it."

"Pray for what?"

"For help."

He smiled and gently touched my knee. "And then?"

"A drunk stepped out of the crowd on Fifth Avenue and blocked my way. He was an odd one. He wore a beaten-up red beret, a filthy jogging suit, and dirty tennis shoes. The bum put out his hand and asked for a dollar so he could go home to his family on Staten Island.

"I stepped to one side, avoided the bum, and walked on. A few moments later a big light exploded in my head. Sweet Jesus, I thought, here I am going to church to pray — and I've refused a beggar! Maybe he needed the money. Who am I to judge?

"I whirled about, pushed through the crowd and looked for the man. I ran up and down Fifth Avenue, but I couldn't find the man with the beaten-up red beret, the filthy jogging suit, and the dirty tennis shoes.

"Inside the cathedral I knelt and asked forgiveness for having rejected the beggar. I crossed myself and slowly said aloud, 'Hello, God, I need to talk with you.'

"I listened with my inner ear for God's reply. I listened very attentively. There was no answer. I repeated my request and again listened. There was no answer. I left the pew, walked nearer to the altar, and knelt before the statue of the Holy Mother. I humbly begged, 'Please, forgive me.' I continued begging. I begged again. But there was no answer.

"Ashamed, but also disappointed, I decided to walk home, drizzle or no drizzle. On the way, I swore to God I'd never again refuse a beggar — even a drunken bum. I remembered suddenly that Sheila had told me I made her beg for everything and then turned her down. I thought that when I got home, I'd start being more generous. I'd begin by being courteous and cooperative with Sheila's group; and later I'd apologize for my behavior about the television.

"About ten blocks from home the drizzle turned into a cloudburst. I started running. After half a block, my breath came hard and I remembered my father's heart attack. Then my chest hurt and I had a sharp pain in my left arm. I slowed. I felt weak and dizzy and I couldn't walk any more. I sat down on the curb, my feet in the gutter where a river of dirty water rushed along into the sewer. I sat there helpless, slumped over — in the street under a streetlight — in a cold, driving rain.

"Many people hurried by. They stared at me, but no one stopped to ask if I needed help; and I was too weak to call out. I must have looked like a drunken bum — sitting there with my feet in the gutter; and for a moment I imagined that I wore a beaten-up red beret, a dirty jogging suit, and filthy tennis shoes.

"In about ten minutes, the pain lessened and I breathed more easily. I pulled myself up by holding on to the lamppost. As long as I moved slowly, walking was not too difficult. By the time I reached home, I felt better, but I was panting, perspiring — despite the cold rain — and exhausted. The group was still there. I fantasized that somehow Sheila would know what had happened — that she would leave the group, run out to me, embrace me with love and concern, would help upstairs, put me to bed, and call a doctor.

"From the vestibule I saw the group in the living room. In the center of the group was an enormously fat redheaded woman sobbing and moaning. The other women (including Sheila) stood in a tight circle about her, holding her up, stroking her. Some were saying, 'We all love you, Gilda. We all love you. Everything will be okay.' Others were swaying and chanting, 'Ummmm, ummmm.'

"I stomped into the kitchen, banging my feet. I was jealous of the fat redhead who was getting all the attention; and I, who might be dying, I was ignored. My resolution of a few minutes ago was gone. Now I wanted to destroy the group. I wanted to tell Sheila I was ill. I wanted her to hold me, to look after me.

"On the kitchen table were plates of fancy sandwiches and a bottle of Scotch. Impulsively I grabbed a handful of sandwiches.

"Sheila came out, said, 'Shhh, shhh — that woman's in big trouble — oh, George, for God's sake, those sandwiches are for my guests.'

"I started to tell Sheila I'd just had a heart attack, but before I got the words out, the fat redhead began screaming. Sheila ran back into the living room.

"I took the bottle of Scotch, grabbed more sandwiches, and went upstairs, massaging the numbness in my chest and left arm. I thought, If I'm going to croak, I'll at least have a warm, full belly. I'll get drunk enough to come back down and break up that kooky group.

"But I did neither. I had a hot shower, put on pajamas, and wolfed down the sandwiches and half a glass of Scotch. By that time I felt pretty darn good. I telephoned the doctor and told him about my attack; but when he learned I no longer was in pain and could breathe okay, he told me to go to bed and call him in the morning. This annoyed me. I had another drink of Scotch and went to sleep. That's all I can remember."

"And the next morning?" the bishop-doctor asked.

"The next morning I felt fine. After breakfast I went to see the doctor."

"Where was Sheila?"

"At her lawyer's office. Our divorce hearing was only about a week away."

"What did your doctor say?"

"He said I had a second-degree something or other and that I should lose thirty pounds; and he gave me pills to take if I had another attack."

The bishop-doctor got up and studied the electrocardiograms. While looking at them he said, "During your description of emotional events, your Greek was perfect. Were you born in Greece?"

I told him I'd learned it from my Greek childhood nurse. He asked more about Ilya, and I told him how she'd been my wet nurse from birth; and how when my mother ran off with another man, Ilya had stayed on and for six years had been like a mother. And I told him how Mimi had kicked her out on my sixth birthday; and how I'd hated my father and Mimi for that.

He looked again at the graphs on the tapes and then began asking me questions on many subjects: about my books, about my father, my sex life, Ilya, Sheila, and about Mimi. All the time he was watching the electrocardiograph. Then he had me run in place, and he listened to my heart again with his stethoscope.

When this was over, he spoke quietly and with authority: "Despite what your doctor in New York diagnosed, there's nothing wrong with your heart. In fact, you have the heart of a much younger man.

Your attack was psychological and spiritual — a warning from your brain, your spirit, perhaps from God. But, Giorgho, even though your heart's healthy, you are in bad condition. You have abused your body and neglected your mind and spirit — which is an insult to the God who gave you your body, mind, and spirit."

It didn't seem possible that I had no heart problem, and I told him that I'd seen the electrocardiograph tape in New York and that the doctor had pointed out the irregularities in my heartbeat pattern.

"Giorgho," the bishop-doctor said, "look here." He placed his finger on the tape. "At this time you were talking about your father and the tape shows irregularities in your pulse pattern. Now look, here when you were talking about your successful books, see, the tape is normal. Here where you were talking about your mother abandoning you, there are the irregularities again. Here, where you were talking about Ilya whom you loved, the pattern is normal.

"Do you understand what that means? When an emotional disturbance afflicts you, the body — yes, even the heart — often mimics symptoms of pathologies that do not exist. But enough of that. I tell you, there's nothing physiologically wrong with your heart. You need exercise, peace, meditation, prayer, and caris. Not eros, but caris. You need good food and work. Work is important — but first you must make your body healthy. Maintaining your health is one way of thanking God for his blessings."

He told me that he would prescribe a routine for the next two weeks and would explain it to Maria. He embraced me, told me the session was over and that he'd like to talk with Maria alone for a few minutes; and that I should come back for another complete examination before I left Lesvos, and that I should stop by briefly every day after exercising.

When we got back to the villa it was noon. I'd been at the doctor's for almost four and a half hours. I told Maria I was hungry. She said that we'd swim first and showed me the door that led from my bedroom to the beach. Then, in a commanding tone, "I'll meet you on the beach in three minutes."

I said my bathing suit was in my luggage which was still in her car. She laughed. "We don't wear bathing suits here. Come now, in three minutes."

I took off my clothes and looked in the mirror. Fat, pasty, flabby.

Opening the door I stepped out into the sunshine which was dazzlingly reflected by the sand; and I was embraced by the sound of the Aegean murmuring to a perfumed breeze.

Maria stood there, her black hair tied on the top of her head. She stood there like an old-time Western gunfighter — hands on her hips, her feet far apart. She was stocky, but not fat. Her big breasts hung down a bit, the nipples large and dark. The hair in her crotch, black and coarse, extended four or five inches above her vagina. Her thighs were well-muscled. What a contrast to Sheila! Sheila has long, slender thighs. There's blonde, silky hair on Sheila's crotch, and not much of it; and Sheila has high-standing, fruity breasts with delicate nipples. And oh, the beautiful balance of Sheila's skeletal structure — an anthropologist's dream — bones so well-balanced that if the flesh were to fall off, one felt that the skeleton would still stand there.

Yes, Maria's body, by contrast, appeared clumsy, solid, functional. Maria's mother-earth body sang of race survival, of tilling the earth, of nurturing and protecting the family. I recalled Venus with the same slightly oval stomach, the sloping shoulders, and the breasts with large nipples. Maria has a heaviness; and yet, it is this feminine sturdiness that artists have depicted as the voluptuous female; whereas Sheila, with her square shoulders and flat stomach somehow, at that moment, reminded me of a handsome, effeminate male. It is this effeminate male type of female that today attracts most men sexually. I wondered why.

Maria ran toward the water, beckoning and shouting, "Come on, old man!" I noticed the efficient movements of her muscular body. She used only the muscles needed to move her toward the water. This also contrasts her with Sheila. When Sheila runs, she exhibits undulating movements of enravishment and sexual invitation. She swings her hips seductively from side to side, pulls her stomach in flat, thrusts her half-exposed breasts out. However when one sees her kinesthetically and not sexually, one sees in Sheila an insecure woman who desperately but subtly communicates, "This is the only way I will be noticed. This is the only way I'll survive."

Almost all men see Sheila as a bright, alluring, seductive female. Sheila's body movements and half-smile imply to many men, "Maybe I'll sleep with you if you treat me right." But beneath her seductiveness there's a tenseness, a body-armor of rigid muscles — especially in the upper part of her beautiful straight back.

I wondered how sex would be with Maria?

The water was cold. Normally, I'd have gone in very, very slowly for fear that a cold shock might provoke a heart attack. Ha! I thought, and plunged in. The water was clear, salty, and so cold that it took me perhaps a minute to catch my breath. I took a mouthful, rolled it around in my mouth, squirted it out. I dove under, my eyes open, and, swimming under water, I thought, *What a mother this ocean is.*

Maria swam over to me and, pointing to a promontory about an eighth of a mile away, said she was going to swim to the point and suggested that I join her. I answered by starting to swim in that direction.

Maria took the lead, going slowly. When we finally reached the rocks, after what seemed to be half an hour, I was breathing hard. My arm and shoulder muscles ached. I could hardly lift my arms above water and had to swim sidestroke.

The rocks jutted up like miniature cliffs. I swam around looking for a place where I could climb up. Maria simply reached over the ledge and pulled herself up, then leaned over and helped me.

The rocks on the ledge were smooth and warm. We sat on them, our shoulders touching. My genitals rested on the warm rocks, and I felt a stirring. Maria leaned over, momentarily touched my stiffening penis with her warm hand, and said, "Your prick is in better condition than the rest of your body."

I placed my hand on the coarse black hair between her legs. She removed my hand and said in a kindly manner, "Your stomach muscles should be as hard as your prick, and your arms shouldn't be tired from a short swim."

I put my hand back in the hair of her crotch. Maria stood up and pushed me into the water. She dove in after me and said, "Remember, I'm the doctor here."

When we returned to her house, I went to my room and slept, not dreaming. In a few hours, Maria awakened me and said now we would eat. For dinner: lettuce, onions, and tomatoes, along with feta, olive oil, lemon juice, and grapes.

~~~~~~~~~~~~~~~~~~~~~~~

T oday is my ninth day here, and much of the time has been physical torture. Maria is driving me relentlessly. Starting last Wednesday, she has been pushing me through a program that, for me, makes the U.S. Marines' boot camp–training look like kindergarten. Up every morning at daylight for a hike. We leave the house and go along the beach, up hills, across olive orchards, up rocky ravines, straight overland for two or three hours. For Maria, it seems effortless and she always leads the way, those well muscled legs of hers moving without effort. I stumble along behind, my legs aching, the breath going in and out of my lungs in gasps, the sweat pouring out of me. I wondered, at first, if my body would stand up. But I had confidence in that bishop-doctor. I knew he'd instructed Maria; and no matter how tortured I felt, no matter how I wanted to stop and rest, I thought, By God, all this sweat and work and misery and pain is giving me back my life. Further, it's developing the stamina and strength with which I'll write my book. I'll hang on. Why else am I here?

After the morning hikes we swim, and every day the hikes and the swims get longer and faster. In the afternoon, more hiking and swimming. And every day on the way back, we stop at the doctor's for a brief checkup. He takes my pulse, listens to my heart, and then, after I've rested for ten minutes, he again takes my pulse and listens. Then he nods at Maria and returns to his long line of patients.

But yesterday he asked me, "Giorgho, up there at Mimi's family house, the place you call the orphanage, you said you were unhappy for eight years and then you ran away?"

I told him that was so.

"Can you remember any happy times with Mimi? Any at all?"

"No."

"Was there anyone up there you liked?"

"Yes, I liked Mary, the black maid. When I was upset, I'd go to her and she'd tell me I was a good boy and that she loved me. She was almost a slave to a dozen people, doing their cooking, washing, mending, looking after them, rushing around from dark to dark — yet she was warm and peaceful. Except for Mary the place was hostile, noisy, hateful."

"You remember her well?"

"Yes. Tall, very black, skinny. Kind and loving."

"The others?"

I can hardly remember their names, let alone what they look like."

The doctor nodded his head, indicating that the session was over.

Our meals were small and simple. At first, we had only raw fruits, vegetables, and a little cheese. As the days passed and the exercise became more rigorous, Maria increased the food. First some bread was added, then yogurt and honey, a glass of wine, and, gradually, a few ounces of fish or chicken.

From the beginning, I marveled at the strength and stamina of Maria's body. It is a thing of functional glory. A few days ago I realized that I had gradually begun to send Maria sex signals. She had ignored them all. Even when I "accidentally" brushed my hand across her breasts, she paid no notice. She neither frowned nor smiled. She apparently was concentrating on one thing only and that was getting me back to health.

I knew I was making progress, and I suspected that Maria was pleased with my efforts. However, it was only today that she showed it. This afternoon I swam slowly, very slowly, to the far promontory (perhaps a half-mile) and back without complete exhaustion. As I splashed from the water to the white sand of Maria's beach, Maria placed her hand on my slightly tanned but still paunchy stomach. I tightened my stomach muscles. Maria smiled approvingly and said, "This evening we'll celebrate the beginning of your resurrection. Uncle Andrew suggested it." She said the celebration would be a small feast of roast lamb. Did I like lamb? I said it was my favorite meat.

"The lamb will be fresh," she said. "We'll slaughter it in half an hour. It's an important ritual. Very ancient."

Maria came dressed for the occasion. She wore a red, Greek dress — with her black braids hanging over it. She had picked out a small lamb, one about four months old.

"I'll straddle him and hold his head back," she said, handing me a knife with a long handle and a long blade. "You cut the throat at this point here." She ran her finger across the lamb's throat. "Cut fast and deep. Sever the throat and arteries in one swift cut. If you hack at it, the animal will suffer. Be sure to stand to one side because the blood will spurt several feet."

I told her I couldn't do it. I couldn't kill the lamb, and if I could I certainly couldn't then eat him. I handed the knife back to her, but she refused it. Still straddling and holding the lamb, Maria stood up straight. I expected a sarcastic remark about my lack of manhood. But that did not happen. Maria spoke gently: "When you eat meat, Giorgho, the animal you eat had to die. Someone had to slaughter it. Everything we eat, Giorgho, has been alive and dies for us. We don't eat stones. Whatever we eat, plant or animal, it has to die so that we can eat it. It is death that keeps us alive.

"Because you eat meat," Maria continued, "you are responsible for the animal's death; and you must accept the responsibility for the death of all those living things that support your life. Of course, you personally cannot slaughter everything you eat. In most instances, someone else must kill the beast or harvest the plant for you."

The lamb tried to get away. Maria held him fast, then calmed him by stroking him. She continued: "If you slaughter a few times — brutal as it will seem — you will be conscious of the animal's death whenever you eat; and you will accept the responsibility for its death. Eating will become a holy process, a nourishing process, filled with respect and thanks. If you never experience the slaughtering, if you are unaware that the animal has been sacrificed for you, you cannot be completely alive. The dead meat you eat may provide you with protein, but you will not receive the life essence that you ingest and digest through your brain and soul — not just through your stomach."

The lamb stood still, quietly rubbing his head on my hand — my left hand, which held the knife. Maria commanded, "Cut!"

I slashed at the neck and hardly cut through the skin. The lamb bleated and gurgled piteously and tried to break away from Maria.

I grasped the long knife's handle with both hands and slashed the blade through the lamb's neck until I felt the blade strike the backbone. The blood spurted over my hands, pants, and shirt.

The lamb fell over. The blood spurting diminished and changed to a pulsing ooze. A glaze dulled the lamb's eyes. I dropped the knife and put my hands over my face. The warm blood smeared over my face and neck and I smelled the pungency of it. A pressure of fright, of shame, and of sadness filled me. I began to sob and tried to hide my crying by rubbing my eyes, smearing them with blood.

Maria said, "A man of courage can weep when there's sadness or pain tearing at his insides." She put her arms around me and kissed my cheek, still wet with the lamb's blood.

"Giorgho, Giorgho, and now you must complete the slaughter by butchering the animal."

She showed me how. Following her instructions, I cut through the lamb's underbelly from neck to crotch, pulling out his still warm,

41

wet-and-moving stomach, kidneys, liver, intestines, heart, and lungs. With salt water I washed the carcass and I washed the organs, silently telling the lamb that he really was not dead — that he was changing his form of life to mine and that I would try to make him feel his death was worthwhile.

"The rest I will do," said Maria, "the skinning and cutting up. The cooking we will do together. Cooking the lamb with love is as important as slaughtering it with love, and eating it with love and with thanks."

Together, Maria and I prepared dinner. We had *arni me yiaourti.* The rack had to be boned to get to the eye of the rib. I did the boning, handling the meat tenderly, visualizing the lamb as symbolically alive. I rolled it in fresh oregano, fresh thyme, fresh garlic; and, earlier, when I had plucked the herbs from the garden, I felt a reverence and gratitude for their existence.

We roasted the rib filet and ate it, along with pilaf, olives, artichokes, and fragrant retsina. For me it was an Easter service. I thought lovingly of everything I ate — meat, vegetables, wine — as kin, benefactors; and I ate slowly, chewing well, speaking little, concentrating my senses on the food. I glowed as I felt the life of the food spread slowly throughout me; and I thought, This woman has nourished me. Like a mother she's led me into getting back some of my health and vitality. She's given me loving advice. She's nurtured me.

Maria was quiet and ate slowly, saying the grace during the meal — reaching forth for my hands so that we made a circle; and then I repeated the grace with her.

In silence, we cleared the table and cleaned up. And all the while I kept thinking, Oh, what a woman this is!

In the evening I went to Maria's room and to her bed. She did not object, nor did she welcome me. She remained still, not moving at all. I put my arms around her; and she still was passive. I began stroking her face and then moved to her neck. No response. I stroked her breasts. She breathed deeply once or twice and raised her chest. I knew I was on the right track and continued stroking her, moving slowly downward. I kissed her. She moved close, put her arms around me, and made soft sounds.

I watched Maria. Her eyes were closed. I watched the long, slow pelvic thrust of her, the undulating of all her muscles — even her arms and hands undulated as she moved them about me, caressing me. Her face radiated pleasure; and when she began to spasm and moan, the great volcano erupted within me too.

After a few minutes of quietness, I withdrew and rolled over. I lay on my back, looking at the ceiling; and I compared Maria with Sheila and other sex partners I've had. While I was thinking about this, I fell asleep.

Maria awakened me. Cooing with affection, she climbed on top of me. She kneeled, straddling my legs. She laughed with pleasure, then came forward and kissed me — her mouth open, exploring my mouth with her tongue while stroking my stomach and groin with her hands and wiggling her toes on my thighs.

At that moment this didn't appeal to me. I was sleepy, very sleepy. I lay still, spent, inert, unresponsive. Maria laughed and cooed more, kissed my eyes, my mouth, my ears. Her wet lips kissed my throat, my stomach, then took my penis in her mouth, shaking her head like a puppy shaking a rag, making happy sounds. I lay still because the head of my penis was tender and Maria was hurting me; and I didn't want more sex now. Maria didn't stop. She turned her body around, kissed my toes, then up my legs to the penis again — all the time making noises of pleasure. She sucked so hard that the head of my penis hurt sharply, and I pushed Maria away. She crawled back on top of me and kissed me with vigor on the mouth again, pushing her tongue between my lips and teeth. I untangled us and moved her away from me. She asked me if being loved was unpleasant, and I told her I was very sleepy. She sat up and said in a tone of astonishment, "But you can't go one, two, three, four and then turn off the switch!"

I didn't know how to cope with this, so I closed my eyes and hoped that Maria would go to sleep. She sighed and dropped her body from sitting to prone, sighed again, pulled the sheet over herself.

A variety of confusions seethed within me; but I forced myself to lie still. I was afraid that if I moved Maria might start again.

After what seemed to be an hour, Maria spoke my name and asked if I were asleep; and I said no, I was awake.

"Giorgho," she said softly, "when we met on the plane you were upset and you had a few drinks and you told me much about yourself; and since then you've told me more. Always your women, the ones you sleep with, are slender, beautiful, fair, smooth-skinned, and much younger than you. Always they look like Sheila who looks like your stepmother — what's her name? Mimi — the one with whom your father went traveling, deserting you and leaving you as an orphan. You also mentioned your resentment for your mother, who also deserted you, and your contempt for your father and the fantasies you had about getting even with him and punishing him for the great harm he'd done you."

I told her yes, I'd told her that.

"And so, Giorgho, is it possible that all your life you've been trying to punish your father by cuckolding him? Whenever you meet a woman who looks like Sheila — like Mimi, your father's young wife — you must seduce her? And your abrupt way — isn't this also a way of punishing your mother — or perhaps all women?"

We both were silent for God only knows how long, with me trembling and feeling that Maria's obscenity was unthinkable; yet I couldn't deny it.

"Giorgho," she said very gently, "you don't know anything about making love. You think too much. You're involved with strategy, not love. When you came to my bed you aroused me like a mechanic with a check-off list. Push that, pull this, massage that, put in some grease, shift gears, put the old engine in high. You're a skilled seducer, Giorgho, but you're not a lover. There's no tenderness, no integrity in your sex. That's what you do, Giorgho, you have sex — not make love. Your sole object is to stimulate an orgasm, gain control, and then reject." She paused, reached over, and took my hand in both of hers. "Giorgho, I want to ask you a harsh question?"

I said yes.

"Giorgho, I wonder why you came to my bed? I didn't invite you. I'm not seductive. I don't look like Sheila or your stepmother, Mimi. I'm stocky, not slender. I'm dark, not fair. My skin is rough, not smooth like silk. And I'm three years older than you are. Giorgho, now my question. Okay?"

"Yes."

"Do I remind you of someone? Do I remind you of Ilya? Or perhaps your mother?"

I choked up, but controlled myself by holding my breath.

Maria put her arms around me tenderly and said, "It's all right, my baby, it's all right."

I put my head on her breasts and wept. When I calmed down, she stroked me gently, kissed my cheek, and told me to sleep.

THE TENTH DAY
WEDNESDAY, 26 APRIL 1967
LESVOS

~~~~~~~~~~~~~~~~~~~~

In the morning, Maria and I had a long swim and then a wonderful lunch of cold lamb with fresh mint and chicory. No mention was made of the night before. Nonetheless, what Maria had told me in bed last night penetrated into every cell of me. And the crystals of that information had sharp points. My psyche and pride were bleeding. During lunch I started to ask Maria what I should do. She must have read my mind, because before I spoke, she shook her head, served me another portion of lamb and said, "Everyone must chart his own ocean."

After lunch the bishop-doctor examined me again and said I had made great improvement — though I still had a long way to go — and that he was proud of Maria and me and that I could return to Athens — but I must keep up the health routine or I'd soon be ill again. He said that I must stop feeling sorry for myself; and that I must stop blaming others and, instead, I must strive to live heroically. He put his hand on my shoulder. "You know how to live heroically. From reading your books, I know that. Now do it!"

A quiet evening. Not much talk and we went to bed early, each in our own rooms. My inclination was to go to Maria's room and demonstrate what real lovemaking was like — with an hour of after-play, perhaps. But I knew it would be a fake, just another strategy to soothe my pride and feed my ego. Furthermore, I was afraid that she might reject me.

I couldn't sleep. What Maria had told me was like a great, new searing sun that lighted up every dark corner of me. Maria had spoken only of my sexual performance. But what she had said accurately described almost all aspects of me. There's no denying it.

THURSDAY, BEFORE DAWN

27 APRIL 1967

LESVOS

~~~~~~~~~~~~~~~~

I couldn't sleep so I got up and walked to Hippocrates' healing ground. I sat on a large boulder — the same boulder, according to legend, on which Hippocrates had sat when examining patients. Something about the spot shook me. I felt as if I were both inside and outside of myself at the same time. I could not tell which era, which year, which moment I was in. I imagined that I was Hippocrates and that I was examining a patient. The patient was I.

"Your ailment, Giorgho Adamson, is that you are a fool. An unthinking fool controlled by your negative past."

I looked at the ground and shook my head. I knew that the past is gone and it is dead. Who can be controlled by something that no longer exists?

"No, Giorgho, no. You certainly remember your pain when Ilya was dismissed. You remember Mimi's thoughtlessness. You remember your father's selfishness. You remember your responding to Sheila as if she were Circe. You remember your anger and resentment as a little boy. Therefore, the past exists; but it is true — you cannot change it because it is over and completed. You cannot go back fifty-seven years and stop your mother from running off with another man. You cannot go back and stop Mimi from discharging Ilya; or eliminate your having had affairs with scores of women who look and behave like Mimi; or keep yourself from marrying three of them and ending up with Sheila, who was more like Mimi than Mimi herself. All that is inalterable. However, even though you are the increments of the past, *you* can change. The past cannot change, but you can. That is, after you learn what you are now and what you want to become."

Don't try to remember the ashes of the past. You've already mixed them with too much filth. However the ashes and filth make good fertilizer for growing the new trees you desire."

The sun was up now, and the morning wind danced through the olive trees. The songs of awakening birds said, "Hello! Hello! It's a new and beautiful day." In the distance, the Aegean turned from dark to light blue.

I got up and started back to the villa. I knew that a small physical and emotional change already had been started in me by Maria and the bishop-doctor. I knew it was only a beginning. But I also knew that today was my last day on Lesvos. Tomorrow I'd be in Athens — and on my own. There'd be no Maria, no bishop-doctor, no Hippocrates. I knew that if I were to make headway, I must leap boldly — with my aching, frightened eyes open — into the unknown abyss of my own self. I'd have to chart that vast ocean before I could plot my course.

There may not be much time left; and, therefore, big risks are appropriate.

FRIDAY, 28 APRIL 1967
PASSALIMANI HARBOR

~~~~~~~~~~~~~~~~

I mmediately after disembarking in Athens, I taxied to the quay. The red boat was still there. I made out her name on the flaked, rotten life preserver: *Mitir-Varvaros*, Daphne, HELLAS. The blue-and-white eyes on the bow stared at me seductively. I held my stomach in, threw out my chest, and thought, You old red beauty, you!

The wiry, little man with the captain's cap saw me on the quay. He jumped into his dinghy and quickly rowed the short distance to the landing. Embracing me as if we were old friends, he said, "Ah, I knew you'd come back." Then he shook my hand and drew me toward the dinghy. "Come along, sir. I'll show her to you, sir."

I said that I didn't want to buy her. I didn't need a boat.

The man, smiling, humming loudly, led me into the dinghy. I did not resist. He said, "Of course, of course! Just look. Looking doesn't cost anything. *Varvaros* will enjoy your visit. She likes meeting strangers. You know what *Mitir-Varvaros* means in Greek? It means 'Mother of Strangers.' "

He rowed the dinghy back to the boat, enthusiastically assuring me that *Varvaros* had been waiting for me. He scampered aboard and then helped me up the rope ladder. Before I could even say thank you, the captain pointed to the mast and said, "Look at that. See how strong it is. No gale could dismantle that stick." Nodding his head, he led me midships and then down into the hold. He ordered me to jump up and down and to tap the strakes. I did as commanded.

"See," he said, "solid as Athos. Solid as Gibraltar."

He took me all over the boat, chattering as if I already had bought her. *Varvaros* is forty-two feet long, has a twelve-foot beam; and is seventy years old. Originally she had been designed for carrying gravel and her capacity is twenty-five tons. Later she was converted for passengers. That's when her name was changed from *Varvaros* to *Mitir-Varvaros*.

When we were through with the tour, the wiry captain poured two cups of thick Turkish coffee from a thermos. He gave me one; and after sipping his, he leaned toward me, his eyes half-closed, and spoke with intimacy, with an air of secrecy:

"This boat, mister, is known for her miracles. That's why monks want her. They want to moor her in Daphne as a holy shrine for fishermen and seamen. But they have no money, and I need money badly."

I asked what kind of miracles.

"I tell you, sir, *Varvaros* has done many marvelous things. If you were a writer, you could write a best seller about her. Once *Varvaros* was ferrying twenty-one monks from Daphne to Crete. But the captain — may he burn in hell — didn't stop at Crete. He locked the monks in the hold and continued south, heading for the slave markets of Benghazi. A few minutes later the wind changed sharply — like a slap from God. The mast stays parted, the boom fell, striking the captain on the head and killing him. Also, the falling boom broke the bulkhead of the locked hold. Oh, this is documented. It's in the records of the Russian monastery on our own Mount Athos.

"Mister, there are enough miracles to fill ten books. Another time,

Varvaros was making passage from Istanbul to Athens when her captain, his name was Aristides, noticed that the tiller was being pushed to starboard by some unseen force. The boat kept veering to port. The tiller stayed over as if an angel were steering. Or maybe the devil. Making the sign of the cross, the captain commanded that they change direction to port for a few hours, saying that it must be God's will. Near Psará they found two fishermen in the water. Their boat had been rammed during the night." The Greek straightened his captain's cap. "You see, mister, *Varvaros* always looks out for people who are in need." He pushed his cap to the back of his head and said, "Mister, do you like to fish?"

I said I did.

"This boat will do miracles of all kinds. If you keep your hands off the tiller, she'll steer you to where the fish are. *Varvaros* takes care of her friends. I tell you, mister, *Varvaros* will look after you better than your own mother."

SATURDAY, 29 APRIL 1967

ATHENS

~~~~~~~~~~~~~~~~~~~~~~~~

I am sitting on the wall of the Acropolis overlooking Athens. I have been walking all morning, thinking about the red boat.

I started in the suburbs a little after six — while the night-blooming cereus still were open and fragrant; and I wandered about this city of white houses, fruit stands, flower stalls, clear-eyed people until now, forenoon, when the sun hangs almost overhead like a big, blinding, luminous orange. The rocky hills reflect the Greek light, the Greek vitality, on me.

No wonder the golden age of Pericles blossomed, dazzled forth, in this rocky, barren, tiny country. This land vibrates with all the energies of the universe. I now understand why much Greek philosophy is based on courage and action. It is no disgrace for a Greek to fail if he fights heroically and with purpose. The disgrace comes if he's been passive and has done nothing. A Greek who makes a wrong decision will be forgiven by his countrymen; but one who vacillates and comes to no decision is scorned.

The Greek sunlight is reaching my vitals. I feel strength churning and flexing within me. My fingers scream, "Put us to work! We've been idle for eleven years." I shout back, "Yes, yes! But how do we start?"

I thought about the seductive red boat. Was it an accident that she was moored so close to me at Passalimani? Are the Fates playing tricks on me? Perhaps. Yet, despite my anxiety, I don't have time to vacillate.

I will go to Agios and get the advance money on my unwritten book.

SATURDAY, 29 APRIL 1967
ATHENS

~~~~~~~~~~~~~~~~~~

I paid the Greek $3,000 for the old red boat.

While the Greek was having the boat's papers registered, I mailed Sheila $5,000 from the book advance. I then telephoned her. The moment she heard I was in Greece, she said I had pulled a fast one and that I must be feeling good. I told her I'd mailed her her money and explained the circumstances. That calmed her; and I then told her that I'd bought an old wreck of a sailboat and would be taking off soon to do research in the Greek islands and get myself in shape to write.

She laughed, "You on a sailboat? Look, George, remember how you used to get seasick on Long Island Sound? You better stock up on Dramamine." I told her it was important for my book that I go to Mount Athos by boat in the same way the early monks had gone there. I had to experience what they experienced — or at least try to — in order to write with integrity.

Sheila said, "Well, George, good luck. I wish you success on your cruise and hope you write well and make a lot of money. I know it means much to you to be productive and successful again. Drop me a card once in a while."

After putting down the telephone, I recalled again that Sheila had been with me on my last trip to Greece. We had been in great passion then and had had a wonderful time.

SUNDAY, 30 APRIL 1967

PASSALIMANI HARBOR

~~~~~~~~~~~~~~

This afternoon the Greek took *Varvaros* and me for an
instructional sail. He patiently demonstrated and then had
me do each thing alone:

> Start engine
> Stop engine
> Unmoor
> Moor
> Anchor
> Hoist anchor
> Hoist sail
> Drop sail
> Steer
> Tack
> Read charts
> Take bearings
> Light night light
> And on and on

I've made careful notes on everything, but still it's confusing. *Varvaros* doesn't handle like the fifteen-foot skiff I sailed as a kid. She moves slowly, indeed ponderously. She stops slowly — much inertia in twenty-five tons. The engine, a Swedish one-lunger, is as old as the boat and one hell of a contraption. To start it: A one-inch plug in the cylinder wall is unscrewed and a small dynamite cap inserted into the cavity. The plug is screwed back in. Diesel oil primer has to be pumped in by hand. Then the bolt over the dynamite cap is heated red-hot with a blowtorch. The dynamite cap explodes — pow! This starts the engine — kapow, kapow, kapow! The Greek had me start and stop it a half-dozen times. I burned my hand twice, once on the blowtorch and once on the red-hot plug.

When we finally moored in the inner harbor, the Greek said that my first cruise should be a simple one. He recommended going to Hydra. "Here's where you are now," he said, putting his finger on the chart, "and over here's Hydra. It's easy. Once you clear the harbor, head for Salamis, then turn to port at Salamis. From there, Hydra's an easy daylight sail. You'll have a steady wind. *Varvaros* will take you straight from Salamis to Hydra. Except for an occasional tack, you'll not even have to change course. The landmarks are easy.

"Your only problem will be when you get to Hydra. The entrance is tricky. No big deal. Drop sail and use your engine."

The Greek told me he'd just returned from a long cruise and that *Varvaros* was low on supplies. There were enough to make Hydra, but he recommended stocking up in Passalimani. Cheaper prices. He said that when he went ashore he'd give his friend Spyros, the ship chandler and provisioner, a list of needed supplies. "I'll arrange for him to deliver at five tomorrow morning. You must have an early start — not later than six — to make Hydra with time to spare before dark. Also, I'll have Spyros bring his son as a crewman for you. It's a good idea for you to have an experienced hand on board for the first few days. The whole deal will cost about six thousand drachs."

I told him I could use some help and thanked him.

"Make sure you're ready at five. Spyros is a busy man and won't wait. Okay?"

I told him I'd be ready at five.

"In a few minutes," he said, "I'll go ashore and start my new life. This boat's been my home on and off for many years." He looked about *Varvaros*, his eyes slowly going from bow to stern. Sadly he said, "Well, mister, she's yours now." He took off his captain's cap, put it on my head, shook my hand, and went below.

He returned shortly, wearing an old-fashioned black business suit, white shirt, black tie, shined black shoes, and an old black fedora — and carrying a scuffed leather suitcase. He looked like a nineteenth-century Greek ambassador — except he hadn't shaved.

"Captain of *Varvaros*," he said, staring directly into my eyes, "a final bit of advice. This afternoon you learned that if you're alert it's not too hard to sail. But sailing with *Varvaros* is more than riding a boat from one port to another. More than hoisting sail or putting the tiller over. While sailing in *Varvaros*, you may meet angels, demons, heavens, hells, joys, sadnesses that you never knew existed. I'll give you a few hints so that you won't be surprised or frightened. Sit down. Make yourself comfortable. And listen well."

He spoke for about twenty minutes. Deep, spooky stuff. He spoke slowly and with authority. From the slowness of his speech, from the somber quality of his black clothes, and the sudden incandescence of the man, I felt like a shivering novitiate sitting at the feet of a blazing guru. He gave me thoughts that never before had occurred to me. I stumbled with them. I had to have time to chew on them. I knew I'd have to think about them after *Varvaros* and I had left port and were alone.

SUNDAY, 30 APRIL 1967
PASSALIMANI HARBOR

~~~~~~~~~~

This is my first night aboard *Varvaros*. I'm on deck under the stars. I'm wearing my captain's cap. I'm writing by the dim, mellow light of an oil lantern. I hear the murmuring of the waves and the boat sounds made by my sleeping *Varvaros*.

The oil lantern is flickering out. It's gone dry. I'll drag a mattress up and sleep topside. I'll need a good sleep. Spyros and his son will be here at five — which means I'll have to up at four. Thank God that the Greek is arranging for the son to accompany me. I'm filling my britches just thinking of being alone on the high seas — trying to handle this twenty-five tons of old red boat.

Varvaros is making soft noises with the swells. She creaks as she swings from side to side, pulling on her mooring line. I don't know what she's saying. It's a strange new language.

MONDAY, 1 MAY 1967

PASSALIMANI HARBOR

~~~~~~~~~~~~~~~~~~~~~~~~

I t is 0420 and I am writing this in an open-all-night waterfront restaurant. The four other customers are longshoremen who are discussing the possibility of stealing tobacco from a German freighter that they're unloading.

I ordered the same breakfast the longshoremen were eating; and the waiter brought me a bowl of stew made from entrails — called *patsass* — a peach, a glass of red wine, bread, and coffee. 18 drachmas — about fifty cents. The waiter stared at my captain's cap and asked if I was from one of the boats. I told him yes, and asked for salt and vinegar. He brought them and asked if by any chance I'd bought "the red one."

I nodded.

"So, Seraflougia sold her? Hmmm."

I didn't know the name of the Greek, but what got to me was the way the waiter asked the question. It made me suspicious and I asked if the boat had changed hands often or was there something wrong with her.

"Not that I know of, captain — of course everyone knows she's old; and I'm told the diesel's sticky."

I was surprised and told him it had started easily yesterday. He shrugged. I said that we probably were not talking about the same boat.

"Captain, every seagoing Greek between Alexandroupolis and Gibraltar knows *Mitir-Varvaros.*"

I asked if the old owner had been trying to sell her for a long time. The waiter shrugged again, wiped his face on his apron, grabbed the bottle of wine from the next table and refilled my glass.

"Captain, you talk good Greek, but you're not a Greek."

"I'm American."

He asked me if I knew Canarsie. Sure, I know Canarsie. "Well," said the waiter, "my brother runs a restaurant there. But about *Varvaros.* No Greek would ask questions about her. Every seagoing Greek knows her — she's something like a small Statue of Liberty. When the Cretans needed ammunition, *Varvaros* brought it. When Kazantzakis needed to escape quickly from Akra Tourlos, *Varvaros* showed up." The waiter sighed and said that someday a writer would write a book on *Varvaros* something like the *Odyssey.* Kazantzakis himself had thought about it.

I asked why, if *Varvaros* were so famous, hadn't a Greek bought her — especially since she was cheap.

"She's too old and slow. Greeks buy boats to make money not to be patriotic. If Greeks have money to throw away, they build a church in their village — not buy a boat that was born in the last century and always needs repairs." He filled my glass again. "Captain, what's your name?"

"Giorghos."

"Well, Captain Giorgho, you've just bought our *Varvaros.* A celebration is what you need. You don't pay for your breakfast. I pay for it. A Greek celebration. No charge. When you return to port, I'll charge you double for your next meal — ah ha!" He bent over laughing, turned away and went back into the kitchen.

It's 4:50 — I've got ten minutes to get back to *Varvaros.*

MONDAY, 1 MAY 1967

PASSALIMANI HARBOR

~~~~~~~~~~~~~~~~~

I t's 7:10 and that blasted Spyros hasn't shown up. Am I being completely suckered? But suckered or not, I must make a decision. Shall I wait here for another day for provisions and an experienced crewman, or shall I risk jumping into the abyss — going alone and with no stores? One thing is certain: if I go today, I must leave now or I won't make Hydra during daylight.

The situation is ridiculous — me taking a nineteenth-century sailboat out on a strange sea. Here I am thinking about going to sea in a seventy-year-old bucket that ponderously makes four knots in a following breeze. Like the horse's ass I am, I bought the boat on impulse, without having had a professional surveyor examine her. For all I know the bottom may fall out. Or I may smash her on the rocks fifteen minutes after getting underway. The guy I paid $3,000 to may not even have owned her.

I must pull myself together and make a decision. Okay, I'll make the decision within the next few minutes. Right or wrong, I'll decide what to do.

Varvaros is creaking and groaning. I've put my arm around her red mast and I'm thinking.

I said, "*Varvaros,* shall we stick around here, or shall we go it alone — without provisions or crew?"

She swung in the breeze, moving her bow fifteen or twenty degrees in the direction of the open sea.

MONDAY, 1 MAY 1967

AT SEA

ENROUTE PASSALIMANI TO SALAMIS

~~~~~~~~~~~~~~~~~~~~~~~~~~~~~~~~~

A t 0735 I set off the dynamite cap and the old diesel engine started up just as she was supposed to. I pulled *Varvaros* ahead by the bowline and cast off. We — *Varvaros* and I — were underway from Passalimani.

Varvaros moved ahead. The diesel engine's put-put-a-put put strength into me. The noise from the old engine sounded like Beethoven's Fifth. I held the tiller with two hands, gazed ahead toward the harbor's exit — like Columbus heading from Palos into the unknown west.

Suddenly the engine stopped. The wind began swinging *Varvaros* around in the wrong direction. I pumped the oil primer. Nothing happened. From the dock, I heard someone shouting over a bullhorn, "Hoist sail! Hoist sail!" It was the Greek. He was running along the quay with two other men.

I pulled on the halyard. The sail went up halfway and stuck there. I tugged hard. The sail didn't respond. Although I'd had a lesson in sailing, this square, lateen rig was a stranger to me — a visitor from the past. Cleopatra's fleet used sails like *Varvaros'*. They don't come like this on Long Island Sound.

I pulled frantically, but the half-raised sail wouldn't go up any farther. The loose canvas fluttered noisily. The boom swung back and forth, the sail thundering. *Varvaros* began swinging to the left when I wanted her to go forward.

I pulled the tiller over. *Varvaros* began jerking around even farther. I swung the tiller the other way. Nothing changed.

I thought, I'll drop the goddam anchor and give the goddam boat back to the goddam Greek. What sly demon had tempted me into this venture? Me, who seldom takes chances.

The sail flapped hard now — with a strange noise — as if *Varvaros* were blubbering with anger or grief. For a few moments she moved ahead, then again swerved on a sharp angle to the left. About fifty yards away, the crew of a big yacht scurried to put rubber tires over the side and waved their arms, gesticulating for *Varvaros* and me to stay away.

I let loose the halyard, but the sail remained in the same place — stuck halfway up. From the corner of my eye I saw the Greek running down the pier side. Over the bullhorn he shouted, "Pull both lines! Pull both lines to raise sail!"

I grabbed the other halyard, the one fastened to the end of the gaff at the top the sail. I tugged on both halyards. The sail quickly moved to the top of the mast and, like magic, embraced the wind. The banging and slapping stopped. *Varvaros* responded to the tiller, steadied, and headed in the direction of the harbor opening, a harbor in which, it suddenly seemed, hundreds of other boats were sailing. They seemed so big, so fast, so many I didn't think it possible to sail through.

Four times we barely escaped collision as we headed toward the harbor exit. How those Greeks shouted and swore and clenched their fists when they had to change course or back down! I didn't blame them. I had no right getting underway without an experienced crewman along. I looked back at the quay but didn't see the Greek and his two friends. Anyway, I couldn't have turned about, even if I had wanted to.

But we made it out of the harbor without them; and I felt like the brave and wily Odysseus after he'd sailed between Scylla and Charybdis. But, I thought, don't push your luck. As soon as you're out of the traffic lane, lower sail and find out what's wrong with the engine. The anchorage near Salamis will be a good spot.

Outside the breakwater, I turned *Varvaros* to starboard. My boat, my red caique — painted bloodred for courage and boldness — made soothing sounds. She headed in the general direction of Salamis, several miles away. Once there, I'd fix the engine and then sail south to Hydra — 31 miles and 12 hours away.

Varvaros lumbered forward on a westerly course, rolling slightly. The sun on the starboard bow reflected off the deck like a great fireball.

'I'm writing while *Varvaros* holds course with only an occasional touch on the tiller.

This is the last page of this notebook. A wonderful moment to start a new one. A good omen? Who knows?

MONDAY, 1 MAY 1967

AT SEA

ENROUTE PASSALIMANI TO SALAMIS

~~~~~~

T he swishing of the waves and *Varvaros'* creaking are the only sounds I hear. The sky is blue, the wind is steady. Historic Salamis is ahead; and on our course there's little boat traffic. This is the first moment of true peace I've had in some time. Also, it is a moment of triumph; and I am getting satisfaction from inspecting *Varvaros*. She's cluttered with gear and boxes; and is bloodred — every square inch of her — except the blue and white eyes on the bow. The Greek painted her. I still don't know his name. It's written on the bill of sale, but I can't make it out. He's a strange one, that little Greek captain. Yesterday afternoon just before he went ashore, he made a philosophical, indeed, metaphysical speech about *Varvaros*, about mankind in general, and about me in particular. At that time I didn't understand him. But now that *Varvaros* and I are alone at sea, I can think more clearly about what my Greek "guru" told me.

"Red is the proper color for *Varvaros*," he had said. "Red is for courage, and travelers always need courageous hearts. Wherever travelers go there is danger. But, sir, you don't have to go to sea, fly a plane, or ride a train to travel or enter strange ports. Almost every human being travels and is a stranger every second of his life — even in walking from the bedroom into the kitchen."

He scratched his head as if he were trying to figure something out. He said, "In your own heart and brain — which are the foreign lands you travel the most — there you'll find many dangers and mischievous strangers."

He waved his arms and moved his shoulders back and forth as if, in desperation, he hoped he could explain the mystery with pantomime.

"You think you're happy, Captain Adamson? You may be. But there also may be a fellow inside you who's sad. You think you're honest? Maybe. But in your guts someplace may be a thief. We all have thieves, cheats, and liars in us. Maybe there's a rapist or a murderer in you. Maybe a saint or an archangel. Maybe Satan himself is sleeping in your stomach. Few of us know what's happening inside us. You may think you're a failure. Well, someplace in your brain a Shakespeare or a Kazantzakis may be writing your next novel. Yes, captain, I know you're an author."

Now I listened.

"It's the same for all of us," he continued. "Some of those strangers — who are part of us but whom we don't know — they jump around our insides like animals in a cage. If we don't recognize them and acknowledge them, they'll foul us up like monkeys at a telephone switchboard. They'll plug us into the wrong number. We'll often be in trouble and won't know why.

"But the inner person whom we males know least is the woman in us. Captain, all of us men, even the so-called Herculean males with bull's balls — each of us is part female. And she-who-is-part-of-us, she, usually, is a stranger to us. We don't even know she exists. It's the curse of males. It's your curse, too," he said, pointing his finger at me in a stabbing motion. I felt my jaw muscles tense.

He continued, "Males usually know nothing about the female in their souls — and that includes you, captain. Therefore you neglect her, fail to observe her, snub her. How does she react? I'll tell you. Neglected and rejected, the woman-inside-you turns into a sly, frustrated, and angry bitch. She waits impatiently; and when her opportunity comes, she flies to your brain and whispers words that you believe are your own. She bewitches you. She manipulates you maliciously — and you're unable to make proper decisions with other women of the flesh-and-blood.

"I tell you, if you fail to recognize and become the friend of your inner-female, then you become a puppet. Your inner-female has a universality and is connected with all other females. You know what that means? It means that if you reject or ignore her, you will do things that will make every woman in the world assist your inner-female in making a fool of you.

"Oh, sure, there are many other strangers in you besides the female part of you — but she's the most powerful."

He cocked his head. A faint smile of secret knowledge softened his facial muscles. "Plato told us about this. So did Heraclitus and many others. But I learned it from *Varvaros*.

"Everyone," he continued slowly, "at some time in his life should have a boat. A good boat has many eyes and is honest. If she loves you she'll talk to you on those rare nights when dolphins leap across your bow and there are a million diamonds in your wake; or on those terrible nights when storms pound you and drive you close to the rocks. It's then — when your ears are opened either by wonderment or desperation — that your boat will talk to you, teach you about strangers, dangers, and many other things — but mostly about yourself.

"This boat's seventy years old; she's strong and wise. Some of the things you'll learn from *Varvaros* may give you a heaven you never dreamed possible. Some of the things may terrify you and fill you with shame.

"But *Varvaros* doesn't need red paint for courage. She's gone through a hundred storms without whimpering or complaint. I painted her red so that the color would reflect on me — and give *me* courage."

Sweeping his hand through a large arc to indicate the entire boat, the Greek sighed, shrugged his shoulders, rolled his eyes, and turned his palms upward. His speech was over. His face became neutral, impassive. He was a merchant again. A boatseller. A stranger. He said brusquely, "Here are the papers and your receipt, sir. Good luck. Adios, Captain Adamson." He saluted and said quietly, "I go now. Would you be good enough to row me ashore?"

On the way to the quay, he wiped his eyes and then blew a kiss to *Varvaros*.

That was yesterday afternoon, before my landlubber's umbilical cord was cut. Now *Varvaros* and I are sailing in the direction of Salamis where we'll anchor for a little while, see what's wrong with the diesel, and then go on to Hydra — our first port of call. Tonight, if the Fates don't play pranks, I'll be drinking retsina on Hydra's famous agora.

MONDAY, 1 MAY 1967
ANCHORED OFF SALAMIS

~~~~~~~~~~~~~~~~~~~~~~

For the last eight hours the Fates not only have played pranks, they've given me a swift hard boot in the ass.

I can't start the diesel. All day long, over and over, I've gone through the routine that the Greek showed me yesterday. I cranked the single piston to the top of the cylinder. I pumped in a shot of oil. I put the ignition charge into the glow-hole. I screwed the plug firmly into the glow-hole, using a wrench to make sure it was tight. I lighted the blowtorch, heated the plug until it was red-hot.

The same result again and again.

The ignition charge exploded. The piston went down and up once with a loud chug-a-chug. Then it stopped.

Every time the same way. One chug-a-chug and no more. How did I manage to start it this morning so easily — before it crapped out?

I checked the fuel tank. It's half-full, and it's diesel oil. Diesel oil's all there is on this goddam boat. No kerosene. I can't light the lantern,

72

the running lights, or the cookstove. They're all dry. I tried diesel oil but it's too viscous. There's nothing to cook anyway — there's a can of anchovies, a jar of grape leaves, and a bottle of ouzo. The water cask has about a quart of scummy water.

The situation's not fatal: we're anchored off Salamis near a pile of rocks — close to Psittalia Island which has a few houses and a navigational light. I see no people. The houses must be vacation homes. According to the chart I'm not supposed to anchor here — but when I couldn't start the engine, it was the only near place to anchor where the water's shallow enough.

Salamis is only a mile and a half away — a beach and houses. Probably stores, provisions, water, and kerosene. Also telephones. I could call Spyros and maybe get him to bring the Greek out.

I'm afraid to risk the mile and a half trip. I don't dare move closer to the beach from this anchorage. When I pulled the plug from the engine, I dropped the red-hot plug into my left palm. The palm's badly burned, blistered, black-and-blue around the edges, and swollen.

I can't hoist sail and steer the boat with one hand. I can't even get the anchor up with one hand. Of course I could row to the beach in the dinghy. But I can't row the dinghy with one hand either. And suppose I made it? I'd be coming back after dark and might get lost. No. I'll stay here.

The truth is that I don't know what to do.

About an hour and a half ago a man in a motorboat landed at Psittalia. He appeared to be checking navigational aids. Later he brought his official Greek boat alongside *Varvaros* and in a high-pitched, bureaucratic manner began scolding me for anchoring in restricted waters. I told him I didn't speak Greek. He shifted to English and ordered me to move elsewhere. I said I'd move as soon as possible. Okay, he said, as soon as you can.

I should have told him my anchoring was an emergency and would he help me because I couldn't move until I had medicine and bandages for my hand, had kerosene, water, food — and got the diesel working. But I was ashamed of being in this mess; and I was proud; and I didn't like the man's arrogance. I didn't like his looks. I didn't like his whiny, official tone of voice. I could make it on my own without assistance from him. I was, in short, a goddam fool.

Now I don't know what to do. My hand throbs with pain. It's festering. I wonder if I have a fever. Yesterday it never occurred to me to ask the Greek if he had a first-aid locker. Now I've looked. Only empty ouzo and retsina bottles in the emergency locker. Not even aspirin.

Here we are in a harbor made famous by Greek heroes, and I'm helpless — paralyzed by pride, stupidity, and an injured hand. What would a Greek hero do? He'd take action. Even if it were a mistake.

Stop thinking and feeling sorry for yourself. Stop waiting for help. Take some kind of action.

There's a bottle of ouzo below. That's an action I can take. I'll have a few slugs of Greece's ninety-proof bottled sunshine. I hear it's great for burned hands.

MONDAY, 1 MAY 1967

ANCHORED OFF SALAMIS

~~~~~~~~~~~~~~~~~~~~~~~~~~~~~~~~~~

I t's evening twilight and I've polished off half the ouzo. I don't mind the pain in my hand anymore. The fact is, I'm numb all over.

Here I am, helpless and fouled up. And drunk. Okay, the great discovery is this: instead of worrying and fearing and complaining, cringing, panicking, I ask myself, "How can I convert this mess into a dazzling success?"

There's a very profound principle involved here. It explains why people voluntarily place themselves in situations of great danger. Are you paying attention, *Varvaros?* Your captain, Sigmund Freud, junior grade, is giving a paper on his latest discovery. Where was I? Oh, yes, the absurd human beings climb mountains, deliberately sail when hurricanes blow, go to war, engage in dangerous sports of a dozen kinds, gamble their fortunes away, walk tightropes over Niagara Falls, and so on. They purposely put themselves into hazard and suffering so that they can prove something about themselves to

themselves, perhaps identify themselves with their heroic fantasies —
and hope others identify them in the same way. Sweet Mother, this
is the motivating force of our modern behavior. It's influenced our
values, our television, drama, news coverage, literature, and art in
general. It's influenced our sports. Millions watch dangerous sports
so they vicariously can be heroes.

Varvaros, you will be happy to know that I'm not quoting anyone.
I didn't get this from Plato or Heraclitus or Sigmund Freud. I
thought it up all by myself!

I'll go below for one more little nip.

I'm a perfect example of what I'll define as the Adamson Principle.
Or would Adamson's Law sound better? Anyway, I'm the perfect
example. Here I am drunk and damned hungry. My burned hand is
oozing. My head pulses with fever. I'm on a boat in what I gather
is a dangerous, prohibited anchorage, and I have neither an engine
nor supplies. I don't even know how to sail.

Why am I the perfect example? I'm the perfect example because
I put myself into this situation. I arranged it. I let one of those
strangers inside of me take charge. That vain, blabbermouthing,
seeker of praise, that scared monkey sure fouled up my switchboard.
I knew what the mischievous internal stranger was doing. Of course
I knew it, and I allowed it. I, Giorghos, am a stupid bastard. I allowed
that hero-seeking traveler in my guts to take charge. See, wiry little
ex-captain of *Varvaros*, I, Giorghos, *I* heard your speech about travelers always being in danger. *I* understood you perfectly!

Ah, this is a classic! Do you know where we are *Varvaros?* We're
in Salamis, the bay of Greek heroes. We're in the bay of heroes and
I, Captain Giorghos, am scared and drunk! This is where the great
battle took place. I tell you, *Varvaros*, that was a day! Prior to that
morning the Persians had defeated the Greeks in every battle. The
Persians had been victorious all over Greece. The only military asset
the Greeks had left was their fleet of small ships in this bay of Salamis.
Right here where your anchor claws into the mud was the only
geography the Greeks still commanded — yes, this tiny bay — along

with their last three hundred or so boats — commanded by a politician named Themistocles.

The Persians moved in with an armada of huge warcraft to extinguish the last flicker of Greek resistance. They blocked the far exit and attacked on this side.

So certain were the Persians of triumph that Xerxes, king of the Persians, brought his royal yacht right by us here and landed on that beach where those red houses are. That's where Xerxes landed to watch his fleet gobble up the Greeks.

Over there in that little bay where you see the oil tanks, the desperate Greek captains asked Themistocles, "What shall we do? We're boxed in and they outnumber us ten to one?"

Themistocles raised his hands to heaven and said, "Our best weapon is the circumstances provided by the gods. We must use what the gods have given us."

Varvaros, do you know what the god-given circumstances were? I'll have another nip and then I'll tell you.

The god-given circumstances were that the Greek fleet was in a small, shallow harbor and the small, shallow-draft Greek boats could maneuver there, whereas the big Persian ones could not. Also, the Persians were impatient. They wanted to put on a show for Xerxes and polish the Greeks off in a hurry. So, the impatient Persians attacked through the narrow, shallow entrance where they couldn't maneuver without running aground. The Greeks picked them off a few at a time, sinking over two hundred ships. If we had scuba gear, we could dive and find remnants of the Persian warships.

Salamis was the battle that saved Greece and, some say, Western civilization.

Varvaros, that ouzo's gotten to me! But I'm sober enough to know that, like the ancient Greek heroes, we must take advantage of the circumstances that the gods have given us. *Varvaros*, do you know what our god-given instruments of success are at this moment?

You don't know?

Well, neither do I. Perhaps in the morning, I will.

MONDAY, 1 MAY 1967
ANCHORED OFF SALAMIS

~~~~~~~~~~~~~~~~~~~~

I n about a half-hour it'll be dark. My hand hurts. My whole forearm throbs and is swollen. But at least I've sobered up.

There's a power cruiser heading in this general direction. I don't care who they are — Greek bureaucrats, jet-set millionaires, piss-ant playboys, or what. I'll get assistance from them somehow. I'll swallow my pride. I'll pay whatever they ask. My mission is to get out of this mess, not to glut my ego.

I've waved at them. They've acknowledged seeing me and are heading this way. The cruiser must be doing twenty knots. Her running lights are on (big electric ones) even though it isn't dark yet. A man in a Greek crew-member's uniform is at the wheel.

MONDAY, 1 MAY 1967

AT SEA

ENROUTE SALAMIS TO HYDRA

~~~~~~~~~~~~~~~~~~~~

When the cruiser came alongside, a second man in Greek sailor's uniform jumped aboard *Varvaros* and asked me, in Greek, what was the trouble. I showed him my hand and told him about the other problems. He gave a whistle of surprise, nodded and went back to his boat, returning shortly with a medicine kit and gave me a tube of burn ointment. After I spread it on my hand, the sailor bandaged my hand and wrist. From a bottle he took four pills — very strong painkillers, he said, take one every four hours. Don't take more than that or they'll knock you out. From another bottle, two more pills. Antibiotics. One every six hours.

From the cruiser's cabin a woman called, "Is something wrong? Is that man in trouble?"

It sounded like Sheila!

A moment later she came on deck. It was not Sheila, of course, thank God. But she was Sheila of about twelve years ago — the same body, the same way of moving, the same voice, the same face — almost.

"Hello," she called over, "is everything okay?"

I told her that now that she and her boat had come to my rescue, everything soon would be okay — and I summarized what had happened.

"You poor *dar*ling," she said, even pronouncing "*dar*ling" the way Sheila does. "By the way, I'm Ziggy."

"I'm George Adamson."

The younger Sheila jumped from the cruiser over to *Varvaros*. She took my left hand in hers and, like a doctor, began feeling and pressing on the edge of the burn and wrist, up to the elbow. Her hands were warm and firm and soft — and looked exactly like Sheila's.

While she was examining me, the sailor — paying no notice to her — brought water and filled my cask (after rinsing it out). He looked at the engine, talking to himself as he tried to figure things out. Then, rattling on to me (never looking at Ziggy), he said he knew nothing about the engine. In fact, he said, it was so old he'd never seen one like it, although he understood that they used to be common on caiques about fifty years ago. He said he had no kerosene for me because the cruiser was all electric. Also he had no food aboard. He and his friend had been hired to ferry the cruiser to Hydra for the owner; and they'd return to Athens by steamer. Then he jumped back to the cruiser and had a consultation with the other crewman.

Ziggy told me that the sailors were giving her a lift to Hydra. The boat's owner was having a party to which she was going. She momentarily took both my hands in hers (Sheila's gesture), smiled, and said it would be a good party. Then she inquired seriously why was I going to Hydra?

At that moment, the goddamned monkey in my guts again fouled up the switchboard. That internal stranger took charge. Before logic could interfere, I heard myself say, "I'm going to Hydra to be with you, Ziggy."

She gave me a quick hug and said, "Great! That's fantastic." She smiled warmly. "I have to go to Athens on the ferry tomorrow, but I'll come back. We'll meet in a few days. You be sure to wait for me."

She squeezed my elbow, smiled again, and went back to the cruiser.

The sailor came over and said that he could call Passalimani from Hydra and have someone tow me to the shipyard or have the marina send a mechanic out — although the mechanic might not know about my old engine. He thought for a moment, then said, "Mister, do you really have to go to Hydra in a hurry? If you stayed here overnight, someone surely would come by and help you tomorrow."

From the cruiser, Ziggy waved and called, "Meet you in Hydra."

The sailor acted as if she weren't even there and he repeated his question to me.

I said, "Yes, I want to get to Hydra."

"Okay," he said. "If your engine isn't working, you better arrive there in the early morning. The wind in the outer harbor isn't as complicated then. From here to Hydra's an easy night passage. I've done it a hundred times — in boats even slower than this one. At night it's cooler and there's less traffic. You'll have a beautiful steady wind all the way until you reach the breakwater. I'd like to lead you over, but the yacht's owner wants the boat there before ten tonight. Do you still want to try to make it?"

"Yes, I do."

He looked at my chart and saw the routing lines the ex-owner had penciled in for me, and nodded. He said I'd have no trouble. The night was clear and the navigational aids on the way were bright and easily recognizable. "I tell you what," he said, "I'll tow you to open water — oh, maybe a half-mile or so — to where you'll be out of the lee and into the wind. You can take it from there."

I called to Ziggy, "You want to stay here with me and help me sail *Varvaros* to Hydra?"

The sailor thought I was talking to him. "No," he said, "we've already been paid to ferry our boat over."

Ziggy called back, "I'll meet you in Hydra. Maybe you'll invite me for a cruise?"

The power cruiser towed me into deep water, to a place where the wind was strong and steady — and cast me off. The helmsman shouted, "It's an easy passage. Good wind all the way. We'll keep an eye out for you in the morning."

Ziggy, who was on the fantail, held her fingers up in a victory sign and then went below. The crewmen paid no attention to her — as if she weren't even there. The cruiser's engines roared, and the boat churned away into the darkness.

While hoisting sail, I thought, George, you've done it again.

I knew what I should have done. I should have stayed anchored, gotten a night's sleep, rowed to Salamis in the dinghy in the morning, telephoned Spyros and asked him to come over with provisions and the Greek; and then seen a doctor. After that, I should have gotten an experienced crewman and sailed to Khalkhidki Peninsula instead of Hydra. I should have moored *Varvaros* in Daphne harbor and spent a month in a monastery on Mount Athos — letting my body heal, my emotions cool off, my brain get clear; and getting started on my book. That's what I should have done. But, instead, I allowed an inside-monkey whom I don't know — to cross my wires and connect me to my old friend (or enemy), Eros. And I allowed another stranger — perhaps named Caesar (you must always win!) — to plug another wire into my ego. But never mind, here we are, *Varvaros* and me, enroute Salamis Bay to Hydra. Never mind the burned hand (which feels alright now that I've had the painkiller); never mind the dead engine; never mind my fatigue, my hunger, hangover, and lack of experience. The wind is in the sail, pushing us ahead on course 160°. *Varvaros* is grunting happily as she lifts up and down in the swells; while I fantasize a juicy affair with a replica of Sheila, but younger.

On to Hydra! This is Greece, the land of heroes. We'll cope with anything, even if we get knocked on our asses.

Am I going mad again? Or am I just ecstatic from the strain and excitement? Or am I in a high from the painkiller pill?

MONDAY TO TUESDAY, 1–2 MAY 1967

AT SEA

ENROUTE SALAMIS TO HYDRA

~~~~~~~~~~~~~~~~~~~~~~~~~~~~~~~~~~

T he wind is steady; and I am able to hold *Varvaros* on course, no tacking needed. I have no running lights, but I have my flashlight which I'll use if I sight other boats. Only sighted one so far; it passed about a mile to starboard.

The painkiller continues to hold me fairly comfortable, although my hand and wrist still are swollen, the skin tight, and the palm oozing.

For hours all has been well — better than well, magnificent! I'm getting the feel of it and some of that navy experience in piloting is beginning to surface.

2215: We passed Aegina light on the starboard beam. *Varvaros* is making a little better than four knots. If she continues this way, we'll arrive off the Hydra breakwater about 0530. On the port side I faintly see the flashing light at Fleves — which confirms our position.

2250: Changed course to 185°. This is the long 24-mile stretch. In about six hours we'll be in Hydra! The stars, the ocean, the darkness, the music of waves, the wind, and *Varvaros* all sing to me. However,

I enjoy the situation not so much because of these things, but because of the personal triumph. *I feel heroic.*

Decades of fantasies have become reality. I am not just writing about climbing Annapurna or exploring Antarctica — I am doing it! I and my big red mother of a boat are crossing the Aegean, a sea that for ten thousand years has been made hazardous by mythical creatures. But *Varvaros* and I have the blue-and-white blinking eyes of Odysseus as our forward lookouts and guides. Suppose the blue-and-white eyes fall asleep? Ah, then, like Odysseus, I must tie myself to the mast, prop my eyes open with pegs, and make noises so that I stay alert until the blue-and-white eyes are rested and awake.

Being a hero is a triumphant joy. I, Giorghos, feel as if I am a world champion. I feel as if I've just clouted in the winning runs in the last inning of the World Series — two out, two strikes, and the bases loaded.

This being a world champion, a hero — is this what provokes my compulsion to sleep with only the most beautiful women — the ones desired by all other men? Is this why I have written so many adventure books in which the major characters are dashing, brave, strong, courageous, and successful despite difficulties that would defeat ordinary people?

There's nothing wrong with having hero fantasies — as long as I don't believe them. And even if I am a real hero. I mustn't believe that either. I must accept success as a temporary gift from the gods, a brief magic-carpet journey to Olympus. Even if I am a champion, it is transitory. Soon I will be eating, crapping, hurting, greeding, and fearing just like everybody else, the people whom we temporary heroes are inclined to hold in contempt. Anyway, in the end comes death. Is that why we all want to be heroes — to deceive ourselves that we can be immortal?

Oh, what a grand emotional evacuation that was! I got it all out of me in two minutes. However, I'm conscious that — at this moment — I have everything I want. Enjoy the moment, kiddo, and don't fool around with intellectual analysis. Enjoy!

About ten minutes after changing course, the painkiller wore off. It happened suddenly, like a punch from an unseen assailant. The pain in my left hand is excruciating. It contaminates my whole body. In ten minutes, I've gone from heaven to hell.

I can't find the three other pills. I put them someplace to make certain I didn't lose them. I've looked everywhere. Oh, God!

I found them — in my watch pocket.
I've swallowed one of them.

It's been twenty minutes and the painkiller hasn't taken effect. I'll take another, despite that Greek sailor's warning.

The two painkillers are working. I have a feeling of numbness, but little pain. I am very sleepy — hell, I haven't had sleep for a couple of days. A few minutes of sleep will help. The wind's steady.

I've just lashed the tiller at what seems to be the proper angle. *Varvaros* moves ahead on course. I couldn't stay awake if I wanted to.

TUESDAY, 2 MAY 1967

AT SEA

ENROUTE SALAMIS TO HYDRA

~~~~~~~~~~~~

I was awakened by a hooting, a scream. About a hundred yards ahead of me an enormous passenger steamer — her lights blazing, her siren screeching and wailing — was speeding right at me. I tried to put the tiller over quickly, but I had secured it. I got the line off the cleat and threw the tiller over to port. *Varvaros* began swinging to starboard. The steamer was trying to go the other way. I heard the noise of her engines straining in emergency power.

The huge stem of the steamer missed us by five or six feet. However I hadn't acted soon enough. We struck the steamer glancingly. We bounced off.

The collision knocked me over. I fell back, hitting my head on the cleat. When I got up, the steamer had passed us. I quickly inspected *Varvaros*. No apparent damage, only scraped paint. Oh, what a hardy soul you are, my *Varvaros*!

From astern, the steamer's searchlight shone on us. I held my

86

thumb up in the "OK" sign. After about a minute — probably satisfied that we were afloat and not damaged — the searchlight was turned off and the steamer continued on her northerly course.

We were alone in the Aegean again, *Varvaros* and me. I'd been asleep for about three hours; and I didn't know where we were. I felt what seemed to be warm rain on my left side. It was blood flowing down my neck and shoulders from where my head had smashed against the cleat. It came from a gash just over my left ear. It hurt some, but seemed to be a flesh wound only. Scooping salt water from the sea into a bucket — even as we moved along — I poured it over my head. The salt made the wound smart. I poured several buckets of the salt water over myself; and it reminded me of swishing the salt water into the gutted lamb at Maria's place. I soaked a towel and tied it around my head. The blood stopped. Now the painkillers kept both my hand and my head comfortable.

On the starboard bow in the distance, I saw a flashing three-second light. Looking at the chart, I knew it had to be Nisoi Tselevina — so we couldn't be too far off course. I steadied *Varvaros* on 185°; and then, feeling very much awake, looked ahead through what seemed to be a slight fog for the light on Cape Zourvas, the tip of Hydra Island.

A half-hour later it showed up. When it was abeam, I put the tiller over, bringing *Varvaros* to course 235°. Eight miles to Hydra.

We were on the last leg of our passage. I thought about Greece, the homeland of heroes. And here I was having a hero's adventure — my left hand burned and oozing, my head gashed (and with a bloody towel wrapped around my skull), unshaved for two days, hungry, in pain, piloting in strange waters ("all travelers are strangers and therefore always are in danger"), and I had just survived a collision. However none of these things seemed important at the moment. For me the important and the heroic thing was that I'd soon be making a landfall on *my* island of Hydra. I call it *my* island because it is my first port of call. Also, I know much about Hydra. During my stay at Maria's, I had read its history — both ancient and modern.

Varvaros moved ahead, humming a duet with the waves. The Aegean was dark blue — and *Varvaros* left a phosphorescent wake — a million white and yellow sparks in the blue water. These must be the diamonds the Greek had told me about; and then, as I looked at those diamonds, a school of dolphin began leaping across our bow.

Was *Varvaros* going to tell me about the strangers, the other faces in my heart?

TUESDAY, 2 MAY 1967
APPROACHING HYDRA

~~~~~~~~~~~~~~~~~~~~~~~~~~

I am writing as I am sailing, leisurely and steadily. I am holding the tiller by hooking my bandaged left hand over it, and
I am writing in pencil in my notebook.

Morning twilight is just beginning to show on the starboard quarter; and I am Odysseus coming home to Penelope ten years after
Troy and after being blown this way and that by evil winds, angry
gods, and mischievous creatures.

I was congratulating myself when I heard myself say, "You fool,
you're not Odysseus returning home to Penelope. You're Paris, following your pecker and your inflamed ego. You're approaching
Sparta, piteously bleating for Helen. You're George Adamson, with
your pants aflame, jumping through hoops for still another woman."

I heard my little speech to me — and had a good belly laugh out
of it. I laughed at the reality of it. What else could I do but laugh?

Dawn is here. The phosphorescent wake and the dolphins have
gone. In front of us I see Hydra. The profile of the hills and city is

unmistakeable. "We've made it! *Varvaros,* you and I, we've made it."
I feel as if I am an ancient Greek discovering Hydra for the first time.
I am Columbus discovering America. I am Vasco da Gama discover-
ing the sea route to India. I am Magellan sighting the Pacific after
381 miles in the terrible straits. Yet the reality is that I am a bunged-up
George Adamson after only 31 miles of calm waters.

We'll be there in maybe a half-hour. What will the wind be like
in the outer harbor? Finding Hydra was a challenge. Now — without
an engine — entering the harbor and finding a proper anchorage will
be another. What the hell, engines are a new invention. What Odysseus could do I can at least try. Of course, Odysseus had a dozen men
rowing when he needed an engine.

Through the binoculars I saw the breakwater. The entrance channel appeared about a hundred feet wide. A flag fluttered on the end
of the breakwater. It fluttered straight out the opening. A bastard of
a headwind. I couldn't tack through that narrow space. I knew that
thousands of Greeks had tacked their caiques through the entrance
for many years — but could I? For me was engine power a necessity?
I said aloud, "You lousy, cheating, boat-selling Greek — you and
your lousy no-start diesel!"
What I had wanted to do — to complete this passage into Hydra
harbor — appeared impossible; and every second we were getting
closer to defeat. *Already I was blaming others.* Was one of the malicious monkeys, one of the malicious strangers inside of me, fouling
up my brain's switchboard and switching me away from reality? But
I knew that at that moment I was fully conscious. The reality was
that there was no one I could punish for my difficulty, for my own
incompetence. There was no one to insult, to strike, to bully into
doing the job for me. There was no one except myself to blame. The
facts were that I had no engine, the wind was wrong; and in a short
time I'd either sail into the inner harbor or smash into the rocky

breakwater; or I would have to turn around and go back to sea; and I wasn't certain I could manage even that retreat.

Again I cursed the Greek. If he had had the diesel engine operating, I wouldn't be in this trouble. I'd have been safe in Hydra harbor as of last night. I thought, *There I go, letting the inner strangers foul up my switchboard again!*

I was close to the entrance. The wind shifted. Now it blew in the direction of the stone promontory that thrust out just beyond the breakwater. The wind moved *Varvaros* and me in the direction of that rocky point.

Should I lower sail or drop anchor? No, too deep. Should I try putting about and sailing back to sea? I didn't think we had enough way on to manage that. In the meanwhile we were drifting rapidly toward the rocky peninsula. In about ten minutes we'd crash into it.

I lowered the sail — at least we'd drift more slowly. In desperation, I thought I'd give the diesel one more try.

Working quickly, I unscrewed the diesel's ignition plug and inserted the next-to-last explosive charge. I screwed the plug in. I cranked the piston into place and gave it a shot of fuel oil. I lit the blowtorch and heated the plug red-hot. The charge exploded with a bang and the engine went chug-a-chug and then it stopped. In my frustration and defeat I screamed and swore at the engine and the man who had sold it to me, and I felt like a fool for having bought it. Then I rested for a moment, holding on to the fuel line for support. In back of it was a small valve — the fuel valve — and it was in the OFF position. Yes, and then I remembered the Greek had warned me about always turning it off when not using the engine.

I, Giorghos, me a Greek hero?

I opened the valve. We now were only about 400 yards from the rocks. I again screwed the diesel plug. It still was hot and I was careful — despite my frantic hurry — to hold it with pliers. I put in the last explosive charge, screwed in the plug, and held the blowtorch flame to it.

The charge exploded. Chug-a-chug, and then silence.

I was defeated. Then suddenly another chug-a-chug. It continued, chug-a-chug-chug-a-chug. I advanced the throttle. The engine speeded up. I put the gear control in forward. *Varvaros* moved. I advanced the throttle more. *Varvaros* responded and moved ahead more quickly. I put the tiller over and pointed *Varvaros'* bow toward the breakwater entrance.

We are in the open space of the inner harbor. We are drifting about, waiting for a berth. For a while, I practiced shifting gears to get the feel of *Varvaros* under power. I put the clutch in neutral, then reverse, then forward. *Varvaros* responded slowly but predictably.

Hydra is steep hills covered with whitewashed houses. One side of the hills is in sunlight and the other half in shade. Half of Hydra is gold and half is silver. It is the kind of excruciating beauty one usually sees only in dreams. But this is not a dream. My head throbs and is wrapped in a bloody towel. My left hand is bandaged. And in this wonderful reality my spirit dances and sings. Columbus and Santa Maria have discovered and have sailed into the New World.

Ho, there, *Varvaros*, we're both bunged up and tired. The collision with the steamer must have been painful for you. Well, we'll rest in Hydra for a while. Still, wherever we rest, we must constantly be alert. Travelers always are in danger. That's what your last captain told me.

A woman in red is waving at us as she runs down the agora toward the seven o'clock steamer to Athens. It's Ziggy. I just waved back. She threw me a kiss. *Varvaros* began creaking and quite abruptly is starting to swing — pointing her bow in the direction away from Ziggy. Is *Varvaros* trying to tell me something? Hold steady, old girl, I'll put this pencil down and take the tiller.

The steamer to Athens is hooting its siren and is backing out. I wonder when Ziggy will return?

We're still lying to, waiting for a berth.

It is now seven o'clock, at which time comes the most important event in Hydra's day. It is now seven o'clock and this big beautiful hunk of steep hills is awakening. What an explosion of joy! Suddenly church bells all over the island have begun to ring. Hundreds of donkeys on the agora and all over the slopes are braying. Roosters are crowing. Dogs are barking. People are shouting. Behind me the night fishing boats are returning to port, their horns announcing that they have a catch that will need unloading. The doors of shops bang and clang open. The shops that cluster on the half-mile of the curved agora suddenly are alive. The bakery has opened, as have the vegetable stores, the tavernas, the barber shop, the hardware store, and the scores of other places of business. Already I see people going in and out of the marketplaces. I see two priests opening the stout wooden doors of the cathedral.

No alarm clocks are needed in Hydra.

Look along the curved agora, *Varvaros*. Look at all the boat berths and see who our colleagues will be — about a hundred multicolored caique — your brothers and sisters. *Varvaros*, this is old stuff for you. But for me it's exciting because those boats are the fiber of the Hellenic people. Yes, *Varvaros*, those hustling Greek boats ply among a thousand harbor towns; and each boat is a tiny fortress, a tiny stock exchange of private enterprise. They are the blood and juices of Greece. These boats sustain farmers, traders, bakers, factory workers, politicians as well as mothers in a million homes. These boats pump supplies and drachma throughout every inch of Greece's long, jagged coastline.

Potatoes these boats deliver, and lumber, and condoms, and toilet paper, fish, hashish, artichokes, wheat, soap, cigarettes, and pottery; oranges, ouzo, retsina, and streptomycin. These seahorses of Poseidon deliver anything — never mind what — that puts profit in the captain's pocket.

Without these merchant boats, Hydra would die; for Hydra is bare rock; and whatever concerns man must be imported.

The only homemade product of Hydra is dung. The Hydriots, their donkeys, dogs, chickens, and cats supply the mouths and anuses. All other things for dung making come by caique from other places of richer earth and more skilled hands.

The commercial day hasn't quite started; and the caiques are just awakening. Different colors they are — blue, gray, red, and green, purple, yellow — as if a heavenly prism has broken up the sunlight and different-colored rains have fallen on the many caiques of Greece.

My eyes see bright colors everywhere — in caiques, in stones, buildings, stores, people. My ears hear sounds I've never before noticed. *Varvaros*, each boat mutters differently. Is there a language of boats, *Varvaros*, just as there is a language of church bells? I hear the church bells individually. Big deep ones and small sopranos. Someone told me that there are 89 churches in Hydra — that is, 89 that have bells. I hear all of them. I hear the *clop clop* of the donkeys. I hear the shouting of Greeks on the agora.

My nose, at this moment, tells of a lexicon of fragrances — the fruits, vegetables, ozone, the bakery, retsina, fish.

My skin feels the wind. Hey, Wind, from where have you just come? From Crete? From Africa?

I can taste all these things even with no thing in my mouth. My mind, too, envelops and tastes everything — past, present, future. My mind visualizes Hydra during the war with the Turks. *Varvaros*, see those rusty cannon? Listen to them roar — they're belching fire and cannon balls at the invading Turkish fleet.

I see Hydra before Christ. Mostly a fishing port. The Temple of Poseidon stood where the cathedral now is. My mind sees the blur of Hydra in the future — in the year 2000. What say, *Varvaros*, let's return here on New Year's Day 2000 and help them celebrate?

Right now every organ, every cell of me shouts, "Hurrah! I'm alive! Hurrah! I'm conscious! Hello all my fellow sinews, guts, glands, cells, and bones!"

Life pulses through this happy body. It pulses through my arteries — refreshing every part of me — my big toe, my liver, stomach, *arbida*, pineal gland — all at once! What more can a person experience? Could I endure such joy constantly? How would I know if it was real? It seems impossible to endure and sustain this happy state without having its reality confirmed. We need others to confirm our experiences and our existence. A single star can never know how bright it shines. When confirmation of our experiences comes, only then do we know who we are and what we are. And this confirmation comes only *through others*. Who will confirm me?

What about the strangers who slink like wild animals throughout the inner bogs of me? The other parts of me — the liar, saint, devil, murderer, conqueror, angel, the cunning, sensuous, ever-alert, universal and eternal woman; and all the others — what about them? Do they also have a need to be confirmed? Oh, George, that's the key!

Hey, there, friends down in my guts! Hello! Come up and have a part of this joy. Come up and look at Hydra harbor — it's very beautiful.

I heard myself speak in a strange voice: "Hello there, Woman-who-is-inside-me. Greetings! What's your name? I'd like to know you. And all you Men-inside-of-me, come up into my brain so I can meet you. What are your names?"

I feel like an ancient prophet — with one foot in heaven and the other in rich, warm earth.

A caique has just backed out. A berth at the agora is clear for us. Are you ready to take us in, little diesel engine? Ho there, *Varvaros*, wake up! Don't tell me you were just resting your eyes. I heard you snoring. In we go, *Varvaros*, you, me, and a group of inner strangers

— heck, no, we'll not allow them to continue as strangers. They are our inner friends and neighbors and colleagues who live deep in the labyrinth of us.

Okay, everyone, watch *Varvaros* and me. We're going in — the Greek at the agora is beckoning for us to enter our berth.

We made it!

Our landing was no thing of beauty, but we made it without hitting other boats and without ramming the seawall too hard. I secured our mooring lines through the iron rings of the agora seawall. I'm back on the fantail now. I have to sit for a while and do nothing except collect myself. Just sit, smoke my pipe and write this. On our right is a caique with baskets of fresh vegetables piled high on her deck. On our left is a caique with kegs of retsina.

Soon after we secured our lines, I heard the crew of the vegetable caique talking about us.

"So the red one's here again with a new owner!"

"He's more dead than alive — blood all over him and his left arm looks broken. A fight maybe?"

"The red one's also in need of a doctor. Lucky they've had good weather. Look, the pintle's loose. Lucky she still has a rudder." He continued shouting about what was wrong with *Varvaros*. The sail was ripped, the antenna broken, the stays loose, the engine sounded bad. On and on.

"Look! Look! They've had a collision," bellowed a man from the retsina caique on the other side. The three on the vegetable caique jumped to the agora, ran over to see for themselves.

"Maybe broke a strake."

"Good paint job! Very good paint job!" said one scornfully, and the Greeks all laughed.

"You think the crazy guy's English?"

"Hey, mister!" one of them called to me in English. "You speak English? You an Englishman?"

I waved at him, smiled, and answered in English, "American."

I didn't want them to know I spoke Greek or they'd shut up and I'd not learn anything more about *Varvaros*.

The Greeks had a conference. The one who spoke English looked at me. "The captain says you should see the doctor."

I nodded and said I felt very bad, and that I had gotten hurt when we'd collided with a steamer.

Another conference, and then the captain called, "Toni! You, Toni!"

A Greek boy trotted over and the captain spoke with him. The boy, about ten years old, jumped aboard *Varvaros* and came to me.

The boy asked me, "You speak English?"

I nodded.

"I," he said, very slowly, "am learning English. I help my father in store. Tourists speak English. Captain says take you to doctor. First I tell my father. In thirty minutes I take you to doctor."

TUESDAY, 2 MAY 1967
HYDRA

~~~~~~~~~~~~~~

D r. Pappas put four stitches in my scalp wound and said that if I'd hit my head on the cleat at a slightly different angle I'd have been killed. He cut the infected skin from my hand, dressed the wounds, shot me full of antibiotics, and gave me sedatives. He insisted that I stay at his dispensary overnight; and he has arranged for me to go to Athens tomorrow for head x-rays and a general checkup. The hydrofoil departs Hydra for Athens at 0800.

It's very pleasant for me to be in a small, good hospital (if I'm not in pain). The hospital permits me to stay in bed without feeling guilty. I can neglect my chores and duties. Someone looks after my basic needs; and I can be comfortable on clean sheets while I daydream, think, or sleep.

As I lay here thinking — then dozing, then thinking more, the same unanswerable questions continued to tumble about my mind as they have tumbled about my mind for many years. Why do I so often reject those things that are good for me; and, instead, I embrace the bad and destructive? Usually I'm not even aware of what I'm doing. I am an unconscious automaton!

Why? Because I've been numbed and conditioned and trained by events in my past. Yet I don't know for certain that the recalled events (when I recall them) ever happened. It's possible that I deviously and devilishly create false recollections in order to satisfy my ego-appetites; or to slur over the present reality or perhaps to assist in my emotional survival.

My recollections of myself (and others) are blurred, nebulous. My memory (both conscious and unconscious) distorts, leaves out, and adds on all sorts of useless, fanciful, often destructive bric-a-brac that confounds the validity of myself. I permit my obscure, often imaginary, past to be a ghoul that feeds upon and despoils my present life.

Can this situation be rectified? Perhaps, if I concentrate on reality; and understand that the only certain reality is *this moment*. The "Now" is the only part of my life that I can learn to observe objectively. And yet as I write this, the "Now" I have just mentioned already has become the indefinite and hazy past.

THURSDAY, 4 MAY 1967
HYDRA

~~~~~~~~~~~~~~~~~~~~~~~~

I took the hydrofoil to Athens early yesterday morning and had my head x-rayed at the hospital. My skull is not fractured; however the doctor warned me that my general physical condition is poor; and he advised me to lose at least twenty pounds, exercise regularly, eat properly, stop smoking and cut out alcohol. He instructed me to rest in Hydra for a week or two, swim as much as possible, and, of course, change the bandages frequently.

On the way back from Athens, the boat passed close to Aegina. That's where Nikos Kazantzakis once lived and that's where he wrote *Zorba the Greek*. Kazantzakis thought mostly about being fully alive in every moment and being free in every moment. These are the things about which he wrote. His inner devices held him unswervingly on that course. Can I follow his example?

It took *Varvaros* and me twenty-four hours to sail from Passalimani to Hydra. The hydrofoil did it in under an hour.

When I disembarked from the hydrofoil, one of the fishermen gave me the bad news on *Varvaros*. The captains of other caiques believe the strake where we collided with the steamer may be fractured. It should be examined; and if it is damaged, it should be replaced. They also agreed that the best shipyard with experience and competence on older caiques, which also is the shipyard where *Varvaros* was built, is in Gythion. It's run by an old man named Yannakatis.

I knew that at the end of my rest period in Hydra I should hoist sail and depart from Hydra for Gythion alone. However, I also knew that I'd stick around until Ziggy came back from Athens. And then what? I had had a similar question after I'd first met Sheila. I had known then that pursuing her would be a mistake, but I couldn't help myself. Can I now? Have I changed at all?

While walking from the hydrofoil dock back to *Varvaros* I realized that, except for changing clothes before I left for the hospital in Athens, I hadn't been aboard *Varvaros* since arriving in Hydra. And I also realized I hadn't had a good meal in several days. Certainly not in the hospital! So, when I saw a caique piled high with tomatoes, onions, and green peppers, my salivary glands began squirting and I had a great hankering for a Spanish omelet.

One of the tavernas had a sign: BREAKFAST SERVED. Inside, a Greek in bathing trunks mopped the floor. Another Greek, in a waiter's white shirt and apron, sat at a table drinking coffee and reading a newspaper. As he read, he muttered angrily — giving someone hell.

The two Greeks jumped up when they saw me. They dashed toward me, one dragging his bucket and dripping mop behind him; and the other folding his newspaper and stuffing it into his hip pocket — but still muttering invectives that might have been that the Greek prime minister is a fool or that the American president has again been duped by the deceptive French. On their way to me, the Greeks' expressions changed from boredom and annoyance to welcome. They talked almost in unison: "Come in, sir. Sit down, sir. Good morning, sir. You want breakfast? Yes! Good food. Special breakfast."

They damned near picked me up in a cross-handed fireman's lift
— to carry me to one of the tables on the sidewalk.

"Good morning, sir. You want fried eggs, coffee, bread? Special
breakfast!"

Before I replied, the one with the newspaper in his hip pocket
turned to the other. "Okay, fried eggs, coffee, and bread for the
gentleman."

I told them in English that I wanted to see the menu.

"No menu," said the guy with the mop.

I told them I wanted a Spanish omelet.

They both nodded, smiled, in unison said, "Okay," and left.

In a few minutes the waiter returned and put down a plate with
two fried eggs, potatoes, a cup of Turkish coffee, and bread.

Now, I began speaking Greek and said I had ordered a Spanish
omelet and told him what it was. The waiter said he'd never heard
of it but he'd try to make it. I told him never mind, paid the bill, ate
half an egg, drank the coffee, and left. I walked down the agora,
sulking; and suddenly I thought, "Why didn't I speak Greek from
the start?" Perhaps I had a will to be abused. Perhaps I unconsciously
had wanted breakfast to be a mess so that I could be angry and get
some sort of perverted pleasure from failing; and then having the
opportunity to blame someone and make myself feel superior?

I decided to make breakfast aboard *Varvaros*. At the end of the
agora, fishermen were selling fresh herrings. They're famous —
filleted and eaten raw with lemon juice, pepper, and ginger. I considered having the fish. But I didn't have the courage to try raw fish for
breakfast.

I bought eggs, peppers, tomatoes, coffee, onions, garlic, fresh
bread, and olive oil.

When I got back to *Varvaros*, I realized that I had no kerosene and
therefore couldn't light the galley stove; and I got annoyed again at
the Greek who'd sold me the boat; and I wasn't in the mood to run
all over the agora looking for kerosene. With petulance I headed

toward the nearest store intending to buy yogurt, honey, some fruit, and a container of take-out coffee. On the way I met young Toni, who waved and shouted, "Good morning, Captain Giorgho. Doctor Pappas said you're lucky to not be dead." He walked along with me chatting away, half in Greek and half in English. And I thought, Yes, I'm lucky, oh God am I, lucky! Then I felt ashamed for having been rude to the two men in the restaurant and for sulking, and for getting annoyed at the Greek who sold me the boat; and I thought, I had had all those negative thoughts automatically. I hadn't made a decision to be irascible — I unconsciously reacted. It was all so absurd that I started laughing. I said, "Hey, Toni, have you had your breakfast?"

"No, Captain Giorgho."

"Come, eat with me then."

He grinned and nodded. I took him to the fried egg restaurant I had left only a few minutes ago. The surprised waiter said, "Spanish omelet?" I told him no, but let me see what he had in the kitchen. On the stove were a dozen pots. I pointed to one of them and asked, "*Oktapodi?*" He answered, "*Oktapodi pilaffi.* For lunch. You want?"

I told him yes, we wanted two orders of *oktapodi*, bread, retsina, and coffee.

Toni pulled at my shirt, "Captain Giorgho, would it be alright if I had fried eggs and potatoes instead?"

After breakfast I bought kerosene. The store also had a few boating supplies, and I inquired if by any chance he had the explosive caps for starting the diesel. He found a box of a dozen and was delighted to sell them. They'd been in the store for over twenty years. Then back to *Varvaros*.

Tomorrow morning I'll have my omelet. I might even invite a guest. Hydra teems with women tourists — Scandinavians mostly, also Dutch and some Japanese. They walk the agora in droves. Hydra appears to be a cocksman's paradise; and the doctor told me that for middle-aged men, sex is beneficial both for the heart and the prostate.

Further, I'm eager to practice what Maria taught me. But first I must overhaul *Varvaros*.

Tomorrow I'll methodically go through the boat. True, I often buy "lemons" impulsively if I like them aesthetically — even if the darn things are dysfunctional; and then I fix them. Upkeepwise, *Varvaros* is a "lemon"; but when we leave here, the old girl will purr — except for the fractured strake. That's beyond me. Even as I sit here I see a disconnected cable loose on deck. I wonder what it is?

I tracked down the cable. The diesel's hooked up with a small generator that charges storage batteries. The batteries supply juice for an emergency searchlight on the superstructure and also for the radio. It's not a bad radio either, a fairly modern ship-to-shore job. I must have been in a fog of ecstasy when I bought the boat not to have seen all this.

SUNDAY, 7 MAY 1967

HYDRA

~~~~~~~~~~~~~~~~

T his morning the fishermen had another catch of herring; and they told me there'd be only one or two days more of the run. I again considered having the delicacy for breakfast and delaying the Spanish omelet again until tomorrow; but I decided against it. I didn't have a knife sharp enough to fillet the smelt-sized fish properly, and I didn't have the condiments. One needed ginger and fresh lemon; and the stores were closed until after mass. Oh, I was lying to myself! The fact is I didn't have the nerve to try the raw fish.

I made a beautiful omelet and set it out — along with coffee and bread — topside. I was about to dig in when I saw a strange man coming toward *Varvaros*. He was big, about six feet, with a huge chest. About sixty years old and bald, he had the easy stride of a cat; held his head high, and had the arrogant mien of a person who always is in command. He carried an enormous canvas knapsack (almost the same model as mine) with a small American flag patch on the side.

His shoes were shined; he was shaved; and his dungarees were clean.

About twenty feet from *Varvaros,* he stopped in front of a store and began speaking in Greek to some people outside of the store. His strong, deep voice indicated certitude. The man looked familiar, very familiar, but I couldn't place him. Where in hell had I seen him before?

When he was not talking, his cheekbones and lean face gave him a severe, almost cruel appearance; but when laughing or talking his face opened merrily.

When he was through with the Greeks, he came over to *Varvaros* and greeted me warmly: "Good morning, Captain Adamson. A wonderful day! And your famous boat — the other captains told me of her many exploits."

He spoke in Greek — not the kind learned in school, but the vigorous demotic Greek, the speech of the people, the same Greek as I speak — yet his knapsack, his clothes, his mannerisms indicated that he was American.

While the stranger was talking to me, young Toni ran by shouting loudly from the agora, "Good morning, Captain!" He ran so close to the stranger I thought he'd hit him. But neither seemed to notice the other. Toni must have missed him by maybe an inch, but he didn't slow down, just continued running down the agora and waving.

Before I answered, the stranger was aboard *Varvaros,* his knapsack was off, and he was sitting cross-legged on deck. From his knapsack he took two plates and several what looked like saltshakers, a cup, a loaf of bread, an orange, and a lemon. On one plate he emptied the contents of the paper bag — about a dozen herring, some of them still moving.

"Eat your omelet before it gets cold," he said in English — like a king condescendingly giving permission to a commoner. Without saying more, the bald-one peeled his orange, ate it slowly, purring to himself; and, when finished, he licked his fingers. Then he took a shining knife from the sheath on his belt and filleted the herring. The brown, strong hands of the bald-headed stranger squeezed lemon on the fish; then sprinkled them with the contents of his three shakers. He shook the last one carefully.

"Ginger," he said. "I learned this in Japan. By the way, my name's Gregory."

His sovereign attitude, his assumption of superior knowledge reminded me of myself. His unnecessary exhibition of his fluency in Greek also reminded me of myself.

He picked up one of the fillets, bit into it, and chewed slowly, smacking his lips and grunting. "Fish are like humans," he said. "Catch them or buy them; and eat them! Eat them raw, alive!" Then a short bark of a laugh.

All the fish were eaten this way, with grunts and "ahs" of satisfaction. The fish-eating was interspersed with sips of the coffee he had poured from my pot and the slow chewing of bread. When he was through, he got up, poured water (from my water jug) over his hands, and dried them on a piece of toweling that I had hung up to dry.

For the first time since we started breakfast, his eyes focused on me. "Ah, ohh, ugh," he grunted. "Now that I have some fuel on the fire I can start functioning properly. Say, captain, I saw you come in last week. Where'd you come from?"

I told him Passalimani.

He nodded. "I knew you had troubles. The caique captains talked a lot about it. I see your rudder post has two bolts missing. Better fix it or you'll have real trouble. You can't sail without a rudder. You've got to command a boat, tell it where you want it to go. Boats are like people. What's your next port?"

"Gythion."

The brown hand reached into the pack again, pulling out pipe and tobacco. After lighting it, the stranger moved close to my chair, put his hand on my knee. A dirty thought went through my mind.

"Captain," he said, "I'd like to go with you to Gythion."

I stared at him.

"You won't regret it. I know about boats. I'm a hell of a good cook and I pay my own way."

I felt like a snail who had left his shell for a little while; and while out of it, a stranger had come along and asked to share the shell; and now I wanted desperately to get back into it, alone. I thought of parasites who worm their way into a snail's shell, and then eat the snail and keep the shell for themselves. I thought, no one is getting into my shell and pushing me out. Suddenly it occurred to me that perhaps the reason this man seemed familiar was because he was like me — *a user of others.*

I asked him why he wanted to travel to Gythion with me.

"Oh, ho! Look, Captain Adamson," he said, "life's too short to have a chemist analyze every piece of food you put in your belly. If it smells good, looks good, and you think it will make your belly warm and make your tongue sing, then grab the food and shove it into your mouth. If you wait for the chemist's report, the food will be rancid — or you may be dead. Captain, you and your little boat look good to me. I just feel like coming. Life's too short to waste time thinking things out."

He paused, relit his pipe, and continued, "I have an appetite to go with you," he said, looking at me, his face relaxed, a friendly smile flickering around the corners of his mouth and eyes. The smile was merry, but still a cunning and manipulating quality shone, like light seeping out into the dark night from between the chinks of a shutter of a house. You can't see into the house, but there's enough yellowness oozing out to tell you someone is at home and awake. I looked back at him, but said nothing.

"If you're afraid," he said, "I'll respect your fear and push no more. We'll forget I asked you. We all have the right to be afraid of things we don't know about. You don't know about me. You never even knew a guy like me existed. But I tell you, you needn't be afraid — no, not of me — you'll be getting the better part of the bargain. I'm a rare one, I am. No, captain, you won't regret having me aboard."

I replied, "Oh?" Saying "Oh?" is a lawyer's trick. It does not commit one; and usually it gets the witness to tell more.

"Captain, to be candid, you don't know salami from toilet paper about boats or sailing. The way you nearly jibed in the outer harbor was sinful. The way you lost your temper at the diesel was worse. Apparently you'd forgotten to turn on your fuel supply. Must have been the first time you started the old diesel.

"Look at the boat," he said, moving his eyes fore and aft. "Obviously, you bought her from a Greek, and I'll bet this knife that the Greek cheated you.

"If that sail isn't patched soon and the pintle fixed and a general overhaul completed, you'll be sending out an SOS — only, of course, your radio isn't working, is it?"

"No," I said.

"From the way you looked when you arrived, I guess the galley went kerplunk. It seems everything's kerplunk except the new coat of red paint."

He snapped his fingers, then held them out for me to see. "These ten little hunks of bone can do anything — fix motors, sails, radios, play a flute, seduce frigid women, cheat at cards, snip an appendix, cut a throat, pick a safe — or cook the best *bakrois* in Greece. And from the way your hand and head are bandaged, it looks like you could use a little expert help."

The son of a bitch was mocking me, and my impulse was to throw him off the boat even if I had to use a club. But I was afraid of him. I looked down, avoiding his eyes. I was losing control of the situation. Again, he reminded me of myself. I recalled how hard I had worked at being clever and ruthless, doing anything to get my own way. Oh, as I look back at myself — making promises of power, offering camouflaged bribes, manipulating people by chicanery. . . .

He tapped his head. "I'll put my hands and my brain at your service. I see you're proud. Okay, I won't do the actual repairs. I'll just act as your assistant — that is, in exchange for a trip on your boat.

I like the color of her and I like the fear in your eyes. It reminds me of myself a long time ago. By God, I know you're smart, I can see that. But you're afraid." He grinned. "Don't get sore. We're a couple of big boys on a happy Greek island."

I nodded — meaning that I wasn't sore — and, goddam it, the moment I nodded I knew he had me.

WEDNESDAY, 10 MAY 1967
HYDRA

~~~~~~~~~~~~~~~~~~~~~~~~~~~~

T he last four days have been days of progress for *Varvaros*,
but of great annoyance to me. Gregory has been "helping" me repair the boat. He's brilliant; he spotted several
things that I missed, even though I feel I'd have caught them had I
been alone. But I must admit, he noticed them before I did. I couldn't
get the searchlight to light after the batteries were charged. "Have
you traced the cable?" he asked. "Anyone with a microgram of brains
would do that first." Sure enough, there was a break in the cable
inside its casing.

Also, the first morning he saw me writing in my journal and he
asked me what it was; and after I told him, he bellowed with laughter,
held his nose, and asked me for whom I was really writing it. Reaching out for the notebook, he said he'd like to read a few entries —
especially what I'd written about him — and he nearly snatched the
book from my hand. Since then I've kept the journal hidden. Gregory is arrogant, ruthless, and smart; and he has a talent for putting
me down in ways I can't escape. He keeps telling me I'm fearful; and

although he hasn't come out with it, he's implied I'm a coward — that I'm not honest with people. "You didn't want me aboard," he said, "but you didn't have the guts to say no. What you wanted was to use me in repairing the boat and then, somehow, to get rid of me. Well, George, old horse, it's too late. We've made an agreement. I stay aboard until Gythion."

Despite the unpleasantness of Gregory's making me defensive, *Varvaros* now is in perfect shape — except for the broken strake. Everything functions beautifully. The sound of the diesel is sweet music. We cleaned every part of the engine and put in new gaskets. And although I feel harrassed by Gregory, physically he's influenced me. Gregory runs and swims every morning, and I tag along. Oh my, that satyr, that Pan, that Caesar, he's all bone, muscle, gristle, and energy. And he works at it.

I heard from Yannakatis. He's full up and can't take *Varvaros* for at least two weeks. I'll stay here until then.

Yesterday Gregory went to Athens, saying he would be gone for about ten days.

THURSDAY, 11 MAY 1967
HYDRA

~~~~~~~~~~~~~~~~~~~~~~~

I'll have at least two weeks in Hydra and have begun working on the preface of the saints book. The purpose of the
preface is to tell readers why the lives of Greece's greatest
saints should interest them. It's easy to write because the subject
interests *me*. I don't want to be a saint — but I covet their peace, their
consciousness, their stability. The material is begging to pour out. It's
rumbling and jockeying like a spring river with a logjam. I've put a
notice up for a stenographer who can take dictation; I'll need one for
about ten days.

A Japanese woman showed up. About thirty. Dark, flat-faced, very
severe and serious. All business. Homely, peasant type, but with her
hair sprayed with something that makes it looked glazed. She came
for her interview wearing a formless muu muu that hid everything
from her neck down. Sandals. She took shorthand superbly and was
fluent in English. She agreed to the job.

I'll dictate to her from nine to noon. Then, while I swim, eat lunch, and change my bandages, she'll transcribe on my portable Hermes. Her name's Ito and she works for a Dutch importer in Amsterdam. She's run out of cash and no one here will cash her checks — and she has another nine days on her vacation. Her working here part-time will be good for her and *very* good for me. She won't be here until tomorrow. She's doing bookkeeping for the pension owner in exchange for her room.

In the meanwhile, the memory bank from my past trips to Athos is disgorging itself; and I am making progress on the book's preface.

When I am writing well, I can feel a book move in the womb of my mind. I feel I am contributing a little bit to God's aliveness. God, élan vital, whatever you call the collective vitality, can only create through the activity of its creatures, be they molecules in stone or human beings. By our work, by the way we live, by some special quality of our thinking, we tell God who and what It is. To exist, God needs us.

When I believe I'm writing well, my soul screams, "Do it better! Stop intellectualizing! Write from the heart. Let *me* dictate to your pencil-holding fingers." At the same time, my body, aching, creaking from the plunderings of old age, impatiently shouts, "Hurry! Hurry! There's not much time left."

Why the excitement over the saints book? After all, it's a routine job of historical research and reporting. Probably it excites me because this assignment has mobilized my energies, which for ten years have been diluted and scattered; and has focused them on the smoldering end of my pencil. The subject, too, gives me hope for my own existence — observing the lives of a dozen of Mount Athos' saints who, over a millenium, radiated peace and joy and love. True, it's probable that some of the saints may have been scoundrels whose saintly behaviors were vanities and frauds. But the genuine saints, I believe, wrought real peace and joy and love. I'm certain they had pains and defeats and sorrows. But they knew what they wanted and they made it happen. That's the key word, *wanted*. If one knows what one wants and *how* to want it, then the constructive energies will flow.

Most people don't know *what* they want, let alone *how* to want it.

Before Gregory left for Athens we discussed the characteristics of saints; and he scornfully said that there is no inner peace, no love, no compassionate joy on earth; that these things are vain delusions and crazy dreams. The reality, he said, is that in this cosmos it's brute eat brute.

Perhaps Gregory is right. Perhaps inner peace, love, and compassionate joy do not exist. If Gregory is right, I will try to create these things for the readers of my book. My pencil will show examples of inner peace, love, and compassionate joy; and I'll try to have them in my own life — that is, if I can discipline my aging body to support my mind and spirit.

But old age — even with its debilitations, with its low energy levels, short breath, and rheumy eyes — is no impediment to peace, love, and joy. Desire them totally, know how to want them and, ultimately, the desired jewel will be created; and the individual who's created It becomes the jewel. It is then that God, *through us,* knows what and who It is and that It still is alive and functioning well.

It may be a long time before I can create inner peace, joy, and compassionate love in my own life. But in the meanwhile, with my pencil and paper, perhaps I can show how a dozen other human beings on Mount Athos made the grand leap.

I'm wondering if I should go to Athens immediately after Gythion (while *Varvaros* is being repaired), do research, and then return to Gythion and sail *Varvaros* to Mount Athos, using her as a floating hotel while I go to the monasteries, interview monks and look through their ancient libraries. The monk here told me St. Gregory's Monastery has an unpublished letter of St. Paul's. What a coup it would be to break that story!

Once I'm on Mount Athos, I believe I can complete the book in three months. Sheila seems ten centuries away — as if our marriage were only a dream.

HYDRA

~~~~~~~~

I was below writing when Ito arrived at 0830. She showed up in a tight-fitting silky dress. Nothing under it. Whew! The valley of her buttocks showed when she turned around. The dress was so tight that every muscle movement rippled through it; and the effect was accentuated by her high-heeled shoes. A beautifully proportioned body undulated beneath that flat, serious face. She had a skeletal and muscle structure made for survival. Obviously peasant stock, a body developed from hard work on the land as a child. Not softly sensuous, and certainly not my type.

I stared. She sashayed around like a model showing a new creation. I told her she must be out of her mind. Walking around Hydra like that was an open invitation.

"Mister Adamson," she said, "you hired me from nine until three. I'm here half an hour early on my own time; and I know what I'm doing. Look, I'm thirty-one and I know I'm stacked. I've been around. I've worked for a lot of older guys like yourself — maybe not quite as old as you . . . you're about sixty-five or sixty-eight?"

She paused, raising her skirt on one side, exposing the flesh of her lower thigh.

I was staggered. Me sixty-five or sixty-eight?

She continued, very seriously, "To be straight, I came here to help you with your work so I can get some cash. But I know from a lot of experience that if we do it — well, er, you know what I mean — before the work starts — get it over with — then we'll get more work done. We'll both be happier. I don't much enjoy sex. But getting it over with at the start simplifies everything. It'll be quite routine; but we'll be done with it. Then we can work."

Smiling mechanically, she came close, put her lacquered head on my shoulder, brushed my thigh with her hand, and repeated, "So let's get it over with."

Nothing about the scene appealed to me — except the bizarreness of it — and I was annoyed with her for thinking I was ten years older than I am. I was about to burst into temper, when suddenly I thought, this will be a good one to practice the Maria techniques on. Nothing can be lost; and I'll be practicing on a stranger whom I neither like nor dislike.

A damned good idea, I thought. I put my arm around her. She immediately pressed close, like a whore trying to excite a prospective customer, and unzipped me. We undressed and lay down silently. She expertly began doing things to excite me. I told her not so fast — and as she lay there passively with her legs spread apart, I slowly and systematically began to work her over until she began to twitch and move her hips.

She appeared to be vigorous and passionate, but I didn't particularly enjoy it — maybe because it was so easy and mechanical. When it was over and I stopped moving, she said that she had enjoyed it, and now we could get on with the dictation. I said not so fast — and very slowly and gently did for her what Maria had done for me. adding variations of my own and wondering what would happen. It took much effort. I wasn't in heat; and I had an inclination to roll over and snooze. Also, that flat face and lacquered hair weren't too attractive. But I kept at it, kissing her from one end to the other, stroking her, exploring her, talking tenderly. At first she appeared somewhat bored and surprised. After a little while she began smiling warmly. Within about fifteen minutes she began responding with moans and thrusts of her pelvis and with juiciness. Her genuine response excited me — and we did it again. This time it was magical. I was a joyful animal, making noises, *not thinking, not observing*. From the sounds and motions of her, she, too, appeared to be a joyful animal. I thought, God, in my old age I've learned how to make love.

Thank you, Maria.

I knew that at first it had been mechanical, willfully strategic, staged. But then even religious rituals are mechanical when one begins to learn them. Certainly it's true with the mantras and also with the way we, as children, were taught to memorize the Lord's Prayer and recite it by rote. I guess all learning processes start off mechanically.

I wonder what would happen if I were to try my new knowledge on Sheila? on Maria? on Ziggy? Could I do it well and in truth, with spontaneity and joy for both of us?

I dictated to Ito from eleven until one. We both worked well, and no mention was made about our "getting it over with." When I returned from my swim, Ito had her muu muu on and had lunch laid out — fish, rice, and fruit.

SATURDAY, 13 MAY 1967
HYDRA

~~~~~~~~~~~~~~~~~~~~~~~~~~~~~~

H ave established a productive routine. Up at 0500. Jog
mile to swimming beach. 0600 to cathedral for meditation and prayer. 0630 to taverna for coffee (only old
men in taverna then). Think out schedule for day. 0700 Hydra wakes
up. To fish pier for fresh fish. Bakery. Fruit stand. Back to *Varvaros*
for breakfast. 0900 Ito arrives. Work on book outline. 1200 swim. 1300
lunch with Ito in *Varvaros*. Afternoon flexible. Eat dinner in taverna.
2100 to bed.

Toni (I learned he's nine years old and wants to be a sea captain)
has been meeting me at the taverna about 0650 to practice his English
for about ten minutes. This morning he said, "Captain George, what
does *shit* mean?" I told him not to use that word in his father's shop.
But, at that moment, I couldn't think of the Greek word for shit.
Toni was eating an apple. I took a bite, chewed it, made motions of
it going through me, and then I squatted, grunted, and pointed to the
ground.

"*Skata!*" he said. "That's what shit is — ah, *skata!*" He thought for a moment, scratched his head, "Captain George, the apple is red, beautiful, and smells good — like flowers. Why, after it changes to *skata* does the apple stink and is ugly — no longer beautiful like apple?"

At this moment the church bells began ringing, the donkeys braying, the dogs barking, the roosters crowing, and the fish boat tooting — all announcing it was seven o'clock. Time for me to go. I told Toni it was difficult to explain the metamorphosis (a lovely Greek word) of the apple into *skata*. But I'd try the day after tomorrow — Monday.

MONDAY, 15 MAY 1967

HYDRA

~~~~~~~~~~~~~~~

Outline going well.

Ito and I working well in all departments.

Toni came to the taverna this morning and I explained about the apple. Then he told me that yesterday the priest had said that man was made in the image of God. He asked me if I agreed. I told him yes, I agreed.

"Captain George," he said, "if we are just like God, does that mean that God's *skata* stinks also?"

I told him that's a question he should ask his priest.

Ah, these Greeks propose wonderful questions. Toni's question truly is profound. I'll ask the monks about it when I get to Athos.

My hand and head are just about healed, but Dr. Pappas wants me to continue changing the bandage daily, after every swim.

SATURDAY, 20 MAY 1967

HYDRA

~~~~~~~~~~~~~~~~~~~~~~~~~

I to departed this afternoon for Amsterdam. After eight good
and productive days we have become dear friends — no talk
about love or seeing each other in the future.

The preface and outline of the book are completed. There are two
or three pages about each of twelve famous saints who lived on
Mount Athos. In filling out the book, I will describe them before they
became monks as well as after. St. Theophile was a notorious slaver
until he was almost forty. St. Paul II had been a warrior. And so forth.
I'll start the actual writing after leaving Gythion and Athens. Once
I start I must have uninterrupted continuity. There'll be no time or
energy for anything else. Not even for this journal.

Gregory should be back any day now. Also Ziggy.

SATURDAY, 20 MAY 1967
HYDRA

~~~~~~~~~~~~~~~~~~~~~~~~~~~~~~

I've been dishonest in this journal. I haven't noted the terrible thoughts that have been bellowing and echoing throughout my skull. Every day, every night, I've been remembering what Maria told me — that I've been obsessed with cuckolding my father; and therefore have been driven to seduce women who remind me of his third wife, Mimi.

Last night I dreamed about it. A long line of women stretched from *Varvaros'* bow all the way to the fish wharf. They were the women with whom I've had affairs or have married. They all looked like Mimi. The woman at the head of the line and the last woman in the line were Mimi herself. All of the women were waiting to have sex with me. But in the dream I was a little boy, eleven years old, and I was frightened by the way the many Mimis were shouting at me.

I half awakened, not knowing that it was a dream and tried to figure out how to escape. But when I looked on the agora and saw no women and when I looked in the mirror and saw I was not eleven, I knew it had been a dream and was happy with relief.

After I went back to sleep, I had another dream. Again, I was eleven. Mimi (who then was about twenty-four) and I were alone in a house. She asked me what were my happiest moments; and I told her I had been most happy snuggled in bed with Ilya, being cuddled by her, feeling comfortable and safe.

"Come," she said, "I'll cuddle you just the way Ilya did. Take off your clothes and get into bed." I was shy, but I did as she told me. Mimi left the room and returned shortly without clothes and climbed into bed. She held me close and said, "Poor boy, you've never really had a mother, have you?" She stroked my back, held me closer and began kissing me. She stroked my stomach, going lower and lower until she got all the way down, and then she said, "My, my, your little penis is all hard. Does it feel good when I touch it?" I said it did, and Mimi took my hand and placed it on the hair of her crotch and told me to rub it. She began breathing deeply and then manipulated me on top of her and put my penis in her. I remember how wet and warm it was. She asked me if it felt good, and I said yes. She told me to move it in and out and that it would feel even better.

At that moment a car drove into the yard, and Mimi said, "Goddam it, it's your goddam father." She pushed me off and said she'd cuddle me more tomorrow after my father had left. She told me to run quickly to my room and get dressed and added that I shouldn't tell my father about this.

The next morning Mimi and my father left.

When I awakened, I knew I was awake and that the dream had not been a dream but a recollection. It had happened exactly that way, and I had forgotten it until now. And I recalled how I disliked my father, not only for marrying Mimi and causing me to be homeless, but also for interrupting what I childishly thought would be another Ilya experience.

Dear George,

This is to acknowledge that your check arrived. Thank you. I thought it might interest you to know that I'm using a little of the money for tuition in night school and a little more of it to buy clothes to go to work in. I have a job. Both school and the job start on the first of June. Wish me luck!

Marty Deenan went through Athens. I asked her to look you up. Agios told her you were recuperating on the island of Lesvos. What happened to your yacht? How is the book coming?

As I write this, one of the happier episodes of our married life comes to mind. Do you remember our week in Crete and how you made a tape recording of the sounds in the little fishing village shortly after dawn, the sounds of the donkeys braying, the goats bleating, the chickens cackling and crowing, and the church bells and how surprised I was that I hadn't noticed those sounds until you recorded them? That was a good week.

God bless,
Sheila

FRIDAY, 26 MAY 1967
HYDRA

~~~~~~~~~~~~~~~~

In the same store where I had found the explosive caps for the diesel, I found an ancient door knocker — bronze, with the head of Athena on it. A beautiful thing with dignity and authority. It was a classical treasure. It enchanted me and I coveted it from the moment I saw it. There was one place where that door knocker had to be — on my study door! The price was tremendous. I couldn't afford it, but I looked at it as a necessity, and so I bought it.

I've been sleeping topside. Very pleasant. Have had fewer dreams than when I was sleeping below deck.

SATURDAY, 27 MAY 1967
HYDRA

~~~~~~~~~~~~~~~~~~~~~~~~~

Ziggy and Gregory arrived from Athens in the late afternoon. Ziggy flew up the gangplank like a happy swallow and embraced me. She had the fragrance of lily of the valley; and as I felt her breasts press against me, her sexuality swirled around me.

Gregory, chuckling — probably he was laughing at me — pulled Ziggy away and said they were going to the dance that started in a few hours at the Athena Taverna. He added, "Oh, I'll be sleeping on board *Varvaros* tonight."

I watched them walk down the agora, arm in arm; and my dislike of Gregory increased. First he had tried to take my boat; then he had tried to change my life style; and now he was horning in on my women. And as I looked at Ziggy's magnificent rearend swaying from side to side, I hated Gregory and I felt competing energies wrestling within me. I wanted to get Gregory out of my life, and I also craved to sleep with Ziggy. This was one of the energies. The other energy was a new voice of me, a voice within me that I couldn't identify and that said, "No! Please, no." It was telling me that I had to break the obsession to cuckold my father and sleep with any woman who looked like Mimi. I knew the advice was pure and true, but I felt that this would be impossible to accomplish by logical willpower. I'd been in the vise for too long. What was needed was a terrible explosion, a tremendous, perhaps painful, explosion to hurl me through my prison walls.

I looked at Ziggy again and then I rationalized outrageously: perhaps if I had one complete affair, a perfect affair with her — not just a frivolous, hurry-up job — perhaps the obsession would be blown away.

Ziggy turned, waved, and shouted, "See you later!"

Should I meet them at the taverna? It's a tourist nightclub for foreigners, not a real Greek taverna. I don't like nightclubs. Never mind. I want to see Ziggy. I won't stay long.

SUNDAY, 28 MAY 1967

HYDRA

~~~~~~~~~~~~~~~~~~

The dance floor of the taverna was crowded. I saw Ziggy and Gregory on the far side of the room. She wore a simple, tight-fitting, black silk dress. Short, a bit above her knees. It showed off a slender, wonderfully formed figure, long smooth legs and thighs, a flat abdomen, and a straight, straight back. Her breasts jiggled as she danced. Her breasts jiggled, and Ziggy giggled with a cheerful, tinkling sound like a silver flute, and I heard it across the room during low points in the music. Whatever steps Gregory performed, Ziggy followed with ease. She concentrated on him as if she loved him and as if he were the most precious and glamorous man in the world.

Then the bandleader announced that the next numbers would be Greek folk dances; and almost immediately the band began playing them. At first, Gregory did not move. Then, slowly and without insult, he pushed Ziggy about two feet away from him, still holding her hands. He stood motionless, straight, stern, then suddenly started the classic Greek dance. Throwing his hands high in the air, snapping his fingers, he gyrated around Ziggy, his feet moving nimbly and quickly, his torso twisting abruptly but with ease and grace.

Ziggy's laughter stopped. It was replaced by a smile of competition. She had to concentrate to follow Gregory — for he was dancing creatively and perfectly. She caught on quickly. They danced several feet apart; yet the intensity of their movements wrought an intimacy. Gregory's face was like marble. Ziggy had the half-smile of someone who is doing something well.

I wanted that woman. Yet how could I compete with Gregory the satyr, Gregory the great dancer, Gregory the ruthless man of action, Gregory of the lean and well-muscled body? *Also, how could I compete with my growing awareness that what Maria had said was true?*

I pushed my way through the dancers and went to the exit. Ziggy saw me. She left Gregory and came to me. Putting her hands on my shoulders, she said, "Don't go yet. I want you to dance with me, and I want to talk with you after this is over."

I was about to ask her to leave the taverna and come back to *Varvaros*, where we could talk, but Gregory came over and asked what was going on. I said I had to go. I touched cheeks with Ziggy and walked away. Gregory ran after me and said, "Remember, pal, I'm sleeping on board tonight."

I returned to *Varvaros* feeling both proud of myself and frustrated. I was like a temporarily cured alcoholic who has refused a drink yet who craves to get drunk; and who knows he'll probably soon succumb to "one more last drink."

I lay down on the mattress on the fantail, pulled the blanket over me, sighed, and closed my eyes. But I didn't sleep. About midnight, Ziggy and Gregory came aboard. They tiptoed and whispered. They went below and lit the lantern. I thought, Why should that bastard have Ziggy? And on my boat at that!

They moved to the forward end of the compartment. Soon the lantern was out. I heard no sounds. In about twenty minutes, I got up and looked below. It was too dark to see anything, but I heard deep, regular breathing. It reminded me of the way Sheila breathed long ago — before we were married.

I tossed and fretted for most of the night. At morning twilight I looked below again. Ziggy and Gregory were fully clothed, sleeping in separate bunks. I felt relieved and went back to my mattress, pulled the blanket over me, and quickly fell asleep.

I was awakened by someone touching me.

Ziggy, wearing the same black dress, looked down at me. I glanced around the deck. Ziggy put her finger on the end of my nose, grinned, and said, "Gregory's gone." She pulled the blanket back, knelt down, leaned over, kissed me on the forehead. "Did you sleep well last night?" I told her no. She asked me what had been wrong, and I told her I didn't like her having been below with Gregory.

"I wanted you to dance with me and then walk me back to my hotel and talk with me," she said.

"I know that," I said, putting my arm around her shoulder, "but Gregory beat me out."

She came under the blanket with me, close, but propped up on her elbow. I felt her soft breast on my shoulder. She pulled away a little and said, "Yes, I should have spoken to you more directly. I didn't realize how little you know about women; and Gregory is a fast operator; and you're scared of him."

She stood up and said, "Come let's have a swim and then I must get my affairs in order before we sail for Gythion — that is, if your invitation still holds."

"Of course, I want you to come to Gythion."

"Good! Now about our swim. Do you know a very private place? I like to swim nude."

I said, "Did you sleep with him last night?"

"Why do you ask?"

"I was jealous."

"No, I didn't sleep with Gregory," she said, kissing me ever-so-briefly. "Did you want to sleep with me?"

The crew from the caique next to us came by, stopped at the gangplank and said, "Hey, captain, we're going fishing. Come along. Better you catch fish than sit on board alone and moping." It was strange, they hadn't noticed Ziggy.

I told them no. I had work to do. They waved and walked on.

Ziggy repeated her question, "Did you want to sleep with me?"

Before I answered, she smiled and said, "George, what you need is a female guru, a female who's your loving friend. You know what — you're scared to death that maybe a real woman will love you. Is it only fantasies you're not afraid of? From listening to and watching you, it seems as if many women in your life have loved you — but you couldn't stand it. What's the matter? Were you afraid that if you allowed them to love you they would overpower you? But first answer my other question. Did you want to sleep with me?"

The ingenuous, the innocent way she spoke — the gentleness of it — momentarily cleansed me of guile, of defensiveness. I was not afraid to answer with intimacy. "Ziggy," I said, "leaving that taverna last night was a terrible crisis for me, a profound event." I stopped speaking because I wanted to think for a moment. I wanted to analyze the situation accurately.

"Yes," she said softly, touching my hand lightly, "please tell me about it."

"When I walked toward the door at the taverna, I felt as if God and Satan were struggling for my soul. The old me — the me of the last fifty-odd years — desperately wanted to hold you, to sleep with you. Just watching you move, seeing your sensuality and beautiful body excited me to obsession. Also you reminded me of others with whom I've been obsessed. A lifetime of old conditioning screamed to me that I must have you. I craved you as an addict desperately craves his drug.

"But then another part of me — perhaps I can call it 'the new George Adamson' — walked into my brain and sobered me. And with this, I had the courage to leave and return to *Varvaros*. I tell you, Ziggy, it took much strength. But later, when you and Gregory came to the boat and went below together, I fell back into my old snake pit. I anguished and raged with jealousy, desire, hate. Yes, Ziggy, I was crazed with the desire to sleep with you."

"Do you think I would have slept with you?"

"Yes."

She laughed — a charming tinkle, a warm sound of pleasure — not approval or disapproval, not affirmation or denial. Smiling warmly, she reached down, took my hand, pulled me off the deck and said, "And do you know, 'new George Adamson,' as a result of your leaving that dance hall, you now have a friend — me, Ziggy. I admire and respect what you did. Come now, friend, let's swim. The Aegean wants to refresh us, to make love to both of us, to sing a song of our friendship."

As we went ashore she said, "I've never been unfaithful to my man."

I looked at her and blurted, "Then why are you such a cockteaser?"

"I'm not a cockteaser. I'm a joyful woman who celebrates my body and spirit. I can't help laughing, touching, and being joyful with everyone. I know this inflames many men. But it's the men who are polluted, who associate my joy in being alive with possible sex. I refuse to change myself because of them."

She stopped talking, turned, and looked squarely at me. "George, is it possible that the other women of whom I remind you — that you've misperceived them? That you didn't understand them? That you painted them as bad when they well may have been good? Could it be that those women are very much like me? Have you been mistaking spontaneity for frivolity, for licentiousness? Have you been mistaking their spontaneity and their reaching for you as an effort to swallow you, to control you?" She paused, then continued, "Oh, don't answer me. It's too wonderful a morning to think. And the Aegean will wash away our silly thoughts anyway."

She grabbed my hand and pulled me along.

In twenty minutes, we reached the rocky cove. Ziggy climbed down the rocks and felt the water, then clambered back, lifted her dress off over her head, removed her underpants and shoes, climbed back down and dove in. I followed her. We swam about, diving under, cavorting like dolphins. In perhaps ten minutes I was tired and got out. She came soon after. We had no towels and, without mentioning it, we lay down on the flat rocks and dried in the sun. I fell asleep.

I was roused by Ziggy who said that I'd been sleeping like a well-fed baby, smiling and relaxed; and that she had been reluctant to disturb me, but it was time to go. When we were dressed she asked me if I had had a good time and I told her that our outing had been very special.

"Why?" she asked.

"Because I experienced innocence." And suddenly, to my intense surprise, I began sobbing. And as I sobbed I thought, I never cried when I was a child!

Ziggy held me, rubbing my shoulders; and soon I was able to look up at her and smile, even though I still was sobbing.

"This is what friends are for," she said.

We walked back to Hydra, had breakfast, and then I saw her to her hotel. When we got there she said she'd changed her mind about sailing to Gythion with me. She said, "If I'm along it'll be more difficult for you to make friends with Gregory, and that's very important. But don't worry, we'll meet again soon — good friends are never separated."

SUNDAY, 28 MAY, 1967
HYDRA

〜〜〜〜〜〜〜〜〜〜

In my kaleidoscopic and haphazardly jumbled life, I treasure the remembrance of several perfect, illuminating, joyful occasions.

Constantly, it seems, I've struggled for what, at the moment, appeared important; and often I've had triumphs; but on review, these triumphs (and the defeats, too, I guess) all have been transitory. I now realize that I, too, am transitory. During the many years during which I have run, stumbled, fought my way through endless vicissitudes, Time has brushed past me like an unfelt wind that never has touched me — yet has caressed me with wrinkles, creaky joints, loose teeth, darkening vision, a stooped back; and all the suffocating weights of growing ever older.

Yet, however, because the gods sometimes take pity on us, there have been a few joyful occasions that which are uniquely indestructible. Forever they glow in my mind like great living opals. I can recall and visualize them at will. They supply me with strength and perspective. I can turn my mind back and see again the glorious occasions in three dimensions, in four dimensions, in full color, with my sense-impressions magnified and heightened. The sweet smells of those happy moments now smell even sweeter. The harmonious sounds repeat themselves with greater and more melodious music. The tastes I had on those happy days are even more delicious. My conversations are more merry, witty, profound. The silences are more meaningful. The touch of gentle hands upon me, the warm embrace of friendly sun, the stimulation of new snow or cleansing rain, the sweet kiss of the breezes — all these in euphoric remembrance are more sensual, more satisfying, more nourishing than they had been in the perfect original.

No matter what disaster stampedes into my life, I always will be able to recognize and feast on these few precious moments.

This morning, my association with Ziggy created one of those memorable, illuminating occasions.

However, the question that follows is: Could every moment of my life be wonderful and joyful if I but allowed it? Oh, God, is it true that I make my own hells — when heaven is always around me and available?

MONDAY, 29 APRIL 1967
HYDRA

~~~~~~~~~~~~~~~~~~

A caique with vegetables arrived in Hydra this noon; and the captain brought me an envelope. He said it was from his friend Constantine. I asked who Constantine was, and the Greek laughed loud and said Constantine was the man who sold *Varvaros* to me.

Dear Captain Adamson,

I heard from my friend Nicos that *Varvaros* has a broken strake and that you are going to have Yannakatis fix it. Good. He knows *Varvaros* well. I am coming to Hydra tomorrow because I'd like to sail with you to Gythion if you will permit me. I know it's an easy sail to Gythion, but at this time of year there sometimes are unexpected short squalls with high winds and waves in Elaphonisos Channel. Not long, but treacherous and difficult. I hear you are sailing soon and I'll be there tomorrow if I may have your permission to join you.

I'm sorry we missed you when you departed Passalimani for Hydra. But I didn't worry. I knew that *Varvaros* would get you there okay, even if you had no provisions.

Sincerely, your friend,

The man's signature (just like on the ship's papers) is scrawled and illegible.

Every day I've been fiddling around with *Varvaros*. Slowly, my past naval experience is starting to flow up from the dark memory bank — vaguely and in small chunks. The skills acquired in the thirty-knot, high-powered destroyers are far different from those needed to sail *Varvaros* (really a seventeenth-century rig with a nineteenth-century put-put engine). Vastly different. Still, the broad principles have some similarity. The seagoing terminology of my navy days is returning to my vocabulary; and with this comes a feeling for the sea and seagoing problems.

I decided to try to apply my distant navy background to sailing *Varvaros*. The way to do this, I figured, would be to take her out for a day before sailing to Gythion; and while out there, to swing the compass. I found the extra magnets and an old sextant in the hold, and I thought I could remember how to do it. Further, I've been watching the Greeks skillfully maneuver their caiques; and I wanted to practice the same maneuvers in the outer bay. Now that the diesel was working, I felt I had insurance against getting into trouble.

I was looking ahead with pleasure to this adventure; and then, at the last blasted minute, Gregory said he'd come along. He said this as if he owned the boat and I was a hired hand. He made the announcement just as I was shoving off. He must have seen my expression of disapproval because he said, rather condescendingly, that he had a long background in boats and that he would help me out. Before I knew it, *Varvaros* was chugging out — with Gregory at the tiller. As soon as we were in the outer harbor he took bearings and said, "You're damned right — our compass is off."

While calibrating — and it took most of the day — I found many other things wrong. Sticky blocks. A slightly frayed mainsheet. Slack stays. At first I felt good about the way my eyes were beginning to see things in a seagoing way — but that blasted Gregory spoiled my pleasure. Always, as I noticed things, Gregory mentioned them — (as if reading my mind) — before I could speak the thought. Gregory recommended — indeed, commanded — that this or that needed fixing. By speaking my thoughts before I could, Gregory not only was draining my guts, but also, in reality, was taking charge of both *Varvaros* and me.

Earlier this month when I singlehandedly sailed *Varvaros* to Hydra, I was proud of my boldness and autonomy; and even though everything was raggedy-assed, I was the king of *Varvaros* and of myself. Today, in Hydra outer harbor — the landmark of my first real freedom — Gregory started taking command of *Varvaros* and telling me what to do. The son of a bitch not only was crawling into my shell, but he was trying to become both the shell and the creature whose habitat it was. I watched him at the tiller. God, how strong and sure of himself he was. That high-cheekboned face on top of the stocky neck and broad chest made him look like a conquering Roman general. I knew I had to confront him or I'd be lost. I took the first issue that came to mind and told him — rather abruptly and with hostility — that I didn't like the end run he'd tried on the relationship between Ziggy and me.

He roared with laughter and said, "That's crap, George. You're seeing things crooked. I've just been social and friendly — and helpful. You know, sort of a good shepherd."

"A good shepherd?"

He pretended to be serious, but, to me, his smile was a mocking one. "Sure," he said, "the good shepherd's the benevolent guardian of the flock. He protects the sheep from wolves, eagles, and other predators, and from their own stupidities. He keeps the flock together and in safety. You remember the Twenty-third Psalm? 'The Lord is my shepherd, I shall not want. . . .'"

"The good shepherd!" Spluttering with anger, I spat over the side.

Gregory snidely interrupted me. "Captain, one thing you've got to learn is never, never spit to windward."

I shouted back, "So you're the good shepherd for Ziggy and me? Does the good shepherd really care for the sheep? Hell, no! He appears friendly so he can make a profit from the wool or from having the sheep slaughtered, butchered, and sold to the two-legged wolves who eat and enjoy the dead meat."

Gregory said, "Don't drop your shit on my doorstep. If you'd had the courage to take Ziggy at the taverna, she would have left me and would have been very, very affectionate to you and you alone. And you know goddam well that's a fact. No, don't drop your shit on my doorstep. Now what do you think, captain?"

I shook my head but didn't reply.

"George," he said, "you poor bastard, you're like the sheep who baaa and bleat but who don't know what the score is in life. Because I used to be like you, I'll give you some good advice. Now listen — but first we should come about."

We came about, and Gregory continued: "In this world everything is a baited trap. The fruit you pick off the trees is a trap to have you carry the seeds to fertile ground. The sweet kisses of a woman are traps. One of them is to get you to support her for the rest of her life; and the other is nature trapping you to propagate the species. Commerce thrives on traps. Advertisements are traps. It's that way with everything. Both nature and man lure you with bait that looks like it's for your good or your pleasure. In reality, it's a trap to gain profit or survival for the trapper. You were absolutely right about the good shepherd. There is no such thing."

He watched *Varvaros* for a moment, then continued: "What you're struggling for — or why would you have bought the boat — is to enjoy life. I'll tell you how. Stay alert for traps. When you see one, stand to one side and spring the trap with a long stick. Then take the bait and enjoy it. That means you must always have a big stick available. The stick has many other uses besides trap-springing. For example, you can use the big stick for pushing people out of the way or beating them over the head if they impede you." He clenched his right fist, smashed it into his left hand, and said, "Well, George, what do you think of my big stick policy?"

I asked him whether many people don't beat you back with their own big sticks.

"Seldom," he said. "Almost all people enjoy being beaten and bruised as long as they have the illusion that the beating will make them look heroic and get them approval, applause, and sympathy. If the original cross of Jesus were found, there'd be millions of people who'd gladly nail themselves on it providing the world knew about it. Yet these same people would refuse to pick up a hitchhiker or give a beggar ten cents.

"George, it's easy to be a philanthropist when everyone knows about it. But to stalk through the world like a hungry leopard, springing the traps of society and of nature, frustrating the wily trappers and glutting one's self with the delicious bait — ah, that's the sign of being a man and enjoying life."

By now we were almost back to our berth. I knew that I hated and feared Gregory and that I should get him away and out of my life. That was the moment I should have taken action.

TUESDAY, 30 MAY 1967
HYDRA

C onstantine came aboard today with the joy of a father being reunited with his child after many years separation. He noticed every improvement, and his eyes lighted with pleasure at each. "Captain Adamson, you really love *Varvaros*, I can see that. Ah, I sold her to the right person. Oh, you replaced the searchlight cable. Good! That used to give me trouble. And you've renewed that cracked block." And so forth. His exuberance and praise pleased me. He told me, however, that he'd forgotten to warn me about one thing. The life preservers needed replacing. He dropped one over the side to show me. It sank about a foot and then stayed at that level. He said that he'd be back in the morning at sailing time, and he'd bring life jackets — he knew where he could get some and it'd be impossible to buy them in Hydra. How many would I need? I asked him to bring four.

He said he had to go now because today's his name day and he was meeting with old friends from the "caique navy" for a celebration. What time would we be sailing? I told him, shortly after sunrise. "I'll be here, captain, you can depend on that — and I'll bring four life jackets. Yes, I'll bring the life jackets. At this time of year you know, bad squalls can jump out of a blue sky in Elaphonisos Channel. They only last a half-hour at most, but they blow hard. Well, adios. Meet you tomorrow, just before sunrise."

WEDNESDAY, 31 MAY 1967

HYDRA

~~~~~~~~~~~~~~~~~~~~~~~~~~~~~~~~

Because we're sailing today I awakened early — long before sunrise — and felt nervous because I wanted to do well. It was still night, and I went on the fantail to think and write a while; and to consider that heaven is here and available if we only choose it instead of confusion and hell. The dark island and the dark sea were quiet, still asleep; and everything seemed mystical and magical.

Morning twilight soon began to draw its light-blue curtain over the stars, and the earth made waking noises. Somewhere a cock stretched his legs, pulled his head back and gave the order that his hens should leave their roost and join him as he scratched for worms and made preparations for fertilizing future eggs. A donkey brayed. On a boat nearby an alarm clock tinkled. Far away a single churchbell joined it. The wind of dawn rustled and played with the sea, making little waves that whispered along *Varvaros'* hull, "Get up. Get up."

On the stern the quiet was shattered by a rasping voice bellowing in Greek. The angry voice scolded someone. Gradually the angry voice became even louder as it entered an argument. Whenever two Greeks talk it sounds like an argument — even if they are brothers agreeing that their mother is beautiful.

I went aft. It was Gregory whose Greek was so perfect it even included the rasping sound. He stood there, his feet wide apart, his hand waving belligerently, his mouth flopping up and down like that of a hungry crocodile. Gregory stood there shouting at a priest who stood on the agora close to our gangplank. This priest was a colossus with shoulders like granite mountains and legs like oak trees. A great black beard flowed down his chest; and his black hat perched over his black hair which was tied in a knot, added to the man's enormousness.

Gregory turned to me, speaking in English, "This wretched pope wants passage to Gythion."

"I would like to go to Gythion," said the big priest softly in English. "I have something to do there before I return to Athos."

"All these black-robed popes," said Gregory, "are bloodsuckers. They prey on the poor and act like they are Jesus himself. This monster probably eats enough for three!" Gregory turned to the priest, and in English, "Why don't you take the goddam steamer to Gythion?"

"I have no money; and it's God's will I go to Gythion."

"Look, you black-robed parasite, if you're working under God's will, why doesn't God make you invisible so you can go on the steamer without a ticket?"

The priest smiled whimsically and said, "You're acting like an Athenian whore."

"You should know," said Gregory. "Anyway, it's not my boat. It belongs to this gentleman here, and for him the boat's already over-crowded."

"I can sleep on deck."

Gregory shouted, "The monasteries are rich — why can't they give you a few drachmas for boat fare?"

"They disagree with my doctrines and beliefs."

"And what is your doctrine? Yes, my fat dissenter, what's your secret?"

"Man and God are equals and they must help each other," said the priest softly. He looked at me. "It does no harm, captain, to help a fellow man. Sometimes it's good."

As I heard this, I began thinking as a writer. If this priest came from a monastery on Mount Athos, he might be useful to me. Further, his expression, "Man and God are equals and must help each other," was almost verbatim from my book. I interrupted their argument by raising my hand and said "One more won't hurt."

Gregory said, "Well, the least we can expect from you, pope, is to bless the ship and persuade God to chip in with a fair wind."

"I bless *you,* friend," said the priest to Gregory. He picked up his battered suitcase and came aboard. He nodded at me, lay down on the deck; and, using his suitcase as a pillow, he shut his eyes, grunted loudly, and in a few moments was asleep.

This annoyed me. The strange priest had flopped out and gone to sleep without even an "I thank you, sir." But we were shoving off soon and there were many things to do. Suppose Constantine were late? Should I shove off without him again?

Hell, no! I needed the life preservers.

At 6:30 Ziggy showed up to bid us bon voyage. She hugged and kissed Gregory and then me. Then she asked about the sleeping priest.

Gregory said, "We're taking a load of beef to Gythion."

Constantine, carrying a huge, bulging duffel bag came running down the agora. Out of breath and a bit unsteady, he came on board. He was disheveled, had puffy red eyes, and reeked of wine. He had a spasm of hicupping, and he reminded me that yesterday had been his name day and that he had been celebrating with old friends.

I pointed to Ziggy and introduced her. He looked in her direction, rather startled, then looked back at me questioningly. I repeated that this is Ziggy, a friend of mine. He removed his cap, bowed, and said,

"Mister Ziggy, I'm glad to meet you." I then pointed toward Gregory, said his name and that he was sailing with us. Constantine looked in that direction, again appeared startled and again turned toward me questioningly; but a moment later he bowed toward Gregory and said he was glad to meet him. I pointed to the priest sleeping at Constantine's feet and said he was a passenger. Constantine stared at the priest, made a wide detour around him, and came back to me. He whispered, "So, *Varvaros* already has introduced you to some of your inner strangers." He tugged on his ear, scratched his head, put his cap back on, and said, "Well, then I better not sail with you. Don't worry. If there's trouble, *Varvaros* will help you." He hicupped several times, burped, nodded in the general direction of Ziggy and then again toward Gregory, saluted me, said, "I'll meet you in Gythion", and, almost stepping on the priest, went ashore.

When on shore, he turned, beckoned me. I went to the end of the gangplank. He came to me and in a low voice said, "Captain, I advise you to shove off quickly — before there are people on the agora who will think you're crazy talking to your inner strangers — or before the harbor gets crowded." He looked slowly across *Varvaros'* deck and continued, "Remember, only you can see them. The wind's good now. Good luck, friend."

I thanked him.

He walked up the plank two steps, touched *Varvaros'* bow, "Adios *Varvaros*, take good care of Captain Adamson." He hicupped again, waved at someone about a block away, and, the bulging duffel bag still on his shoulder, walked shakily down the agora.

It wasn't until he was out of sight that I remembered the blasted life jackets. I guessed that he had them stuffed in the duffel bag. I ran to the end of the agora. He wasn't there. I asked the crew of the fishing boat if they had seen him. Yes, they had seen him, but they hadn't noticed where he'd gone.

People were beginning to move around the agora, and I heard a few of the caique motors warming up. I hurried back to *Varvaros*, deciding that I'd risk it.

WEDNESDAY, 31 MAY 1967

AT SEA

ENROUTE HYDRA TO GYTHION

Using the engine, I took *Varvaros* out of the harbor. Gregory tried to horn in by telling me how to do this or that, turn to starboard here, slow down there. However, I did what I wanted, not even acknowledging what he said. I knew that I had to regain and maintain command.

After reaching open water, I ordered Gregory to help me hoist sail; and then I checked the plotted course. The wind was steady. I secured the lines to see if *Varvaros* would stay on course by herself. She did. I told Gregory to take over the helm, that no course change would be needed until about two; that I was tired and would sleep until noon; and that he should not change anything without informing me.

Gregory replied to each of my commands with an exaggerated salute and a mocking "aye, aye, sir." But he did what I had ordered.

On my way below to my bunk, I saw that the priest was still stretched out on the deck, snoring like thunder.

I awakened just before noon and came topside. Gregory and a big clean-shaven man — whose head as well as face was shaved — a stranger wearing peasant's homespun clothes, squatted on deck eating bread, cheese, and olives with tomatoes and radikia. I knew who he was; still, I asked, "And where in the hell is the priest?"

The clean-shaven fellow answered, "There is no priest."

"Oh?" I said.

The huge shaved one in his basso profundo voice said, "There no longer is a priest." He paused, lowered his eyes. "I temporarily defrocked myself two hours ago." He put a piece of cheese in his mouth, rolled it around, swallowed it. "Now I can sin anonymously — like the rest of you."

I asked him why he had defrocked himself, and he said that he had been banished from the monastery for six weeks to serve penance for his sins. I asked what his sins had been, and he replied, "I said I could talk with God. The abbot asked me if I was claiming to be Jesus or one of the prophets. I told him no, that all people can hear God at any time they want if they will only listen."

"Can you tell us what God's talking about right now?" said Gregory.

"Of course. But I won't. It's better you learn to listen for yourself." He ran his hand over his shaved face and shaved head. "Now I'm free. At least I'm free from lice." He stood up, grinning, "You won't regret taking me. I don't know the front from the back of a ship, and I can't swim, and I get seasick very easily. But, I tell you, I'll earn my way. I'm strong as Hercules," he said, flexing the huge muscles in his arms. "And these big fingers of mine are nimble as the mainspring of your wristwatch." He tapped his temple with his fingers. "And what's inside this thick skull is even better than my muscles. Oh, I can earn my way alright, friends, don't you worry about that."

Gregory and I looked at each other. I wanted to laugh, remembering that Gregory had made almost the same speech when he had asked to come on board *Varvaros;* however I dared not even smile at that moment.

The colossus continued, "There's nothing I can't do."

Gregory interrupted him, "Except get the boat fare to Gythion, eh?"

The colossus said, "Except get mankind to listen to God's pleading for help."

"If you can't swim and you get seasick," said Gregory, "I hope you can at least walk on the water like Jesus."

I said, "Eat, stranger, and feel welcome."

"If you wish," said the colossus. "My name's Alexis."

No one spoke for a while, and then I asked him who had shaved him. Alexis-the-colossus laughed — as loud as ten bass drums. "Gregory shaved me. In fact, it was his idea. And a blessed good one it was. He said it was part of the black sabbath ritual. I didn't care. Black sabbath, white sabbath, green sabbath, it made no difference to me. I'm on a six-week recreation. I'm free and I fill the universe."

At that moment lightning flashed on the horizon, and about ten seconds later a boom of thunder roared across the sea. Gregory muttered that there wasn't even a cloud in the sky; and wondered what in hell was up.

Alexis pounded his huge fist on the superstructure. "God is grumbling because He's jealous of the likes of us. There are some things man can do that God cannot." He put his arm around my shoulder, "But don't worry, little captain, if the Fates dance on your bowsprit, I'll twist their necks the way one does to a fat rooster before feast day!" He bellowed with laughter again, then turned sharply to Gregory. "And why did you cross yourself when you saw and heard God complain a few moments ago?"

I had noticed Gregory's hand moving oddly. I nodded at Alexis' question.

Gregory denied crossing himself.

"Ah, ha!" said Alexis. "So you were a scared little girl before you became a brassy Athenian whore. Well, there's still hope that you can learn about love."

Gregory scowled and said, "Just what is this love shit, my elephantine, defrocked Jesus?"

Alexis gently answered that love was the most powerful energy in the world, in the cosmos. Gregory held his nose and said he'd give Alexis the facts of life, and with this he made a speech:

"Fear," he said, "not love, is the most powerful energy in the world. Yes, fear is the most powerful energy in the world. For ten million years human beings have been more influenced by fear of some sort than by anything else. Today people drive their cars within the speed limit only because they have fear of lurking cops. People would steal, cheat, murder if they did not fear being caught and punished. What creates ambition in people? For many it is fear of poverty in their old age. Often it is a desire for power, which is a fear of being inferior. What makes war? It's the collective fear that one's nation will lose what it now has; or the fear that the nation will not get what it needs. What makes children tell lies? Fear. What makes adults tell lies? Fear.

"Almost all Christian churches teach doctrines of fear. There is the fear of hell or the loss of heaven after death. There is the fear of not being approved of by the rest of the flock. The same principle is found in Mohammedanism as well as in most other religions. What kind of a god is Jehovah of the Jews? Jehovah is a terrible god of revenge. An eye for an eye and a tooth for a tooth. Religion, then, too, is an institution based on fear. No, pope, you're wrong about love. Fear's the most powerful energy in the world. It's only the weak, the cowards, the frightened who prattle about love. You can get anything you want by making people afraid of you. That's how I got where I am. That's why I'm on this boat — because the captain was afraid to deny my request. Because he was in fear of me. I got where I am today because people are afraid of me."

Alexis said he was not afraid of Gregory and the reason he wasn't afraid was, despite their arguing, that he loved him.

Gregory took out his sheath knife and said, "If I started to carve you up with this, you might change your mind about loving me."

Alexis laughed, "Whether you have a knife or a gun or a platoon of marines, I could break your back with one hand tied behind me. But I wouldn't, because I love you."

Gregory, like a stalking panther, moved slowly toward Alexis. I had had enough. I told both of them to shut up, there was work to do. Gregory told me to mind my own business. I walked up to him. With my face about six inches from his, I said, "This is my boat. If you don't like it, you can go ashore. You can go ashore at the next village." I walked away, and over my shoulder said, "Now, Gregory, get on the radio and tune in the weather station. And you, Alexis, put away the food and clean up the dishes." Alexis asked me if I didn't want to eat first. I told him no.

I was surprised that both did as I commanded, immediately and without resistance. Alexis smiled peacefully, but Gregory had looked resentful. In a few minutes he returned saying the weather report was okay. Then I recalled what Constantine had said about unexpected squalls at this time of year; and I thought, We have neither life preservers nor life jackets, and the goddam dinghy would sink in two minutes in a storm. I felt myself frowning, and then I heard *Varvaros* creaking and sighing as she rolled and moved through the water, as if assuring me that everything would be taken care of.

Alexis began to look woozy. He watched Gregory every moment. When Gregory went below, Alexis went to the fantail and began throwing up.

WEDNESDAY, 31 MAY 1967
AT SEA ENROUTE HYDRA TO GYTHION

~~~~~~~~~~~~~~~~~~~~~~~~~~~~~~~~~

By the time we changed course, everyone seemed happy. Alexis had recovered from his seasickness. We had a blue sky, a warm sun, a calm sea, and a friendly wind. The three of us — all in bathing trunks — sat in canvas chairs in the stern sheets. Earlier, Gregory and Alexis seemed to have made peace; and even had had a civilized conversation about the best ways of cooking tripe. Me, I felt that everything was under control. A steady breeze came over our quarter, billowing the sail into full-breastedness. The patched lateen canvas stretched, held its broad arms wide, and snared the wind — which pushed *Varvaros* at about four knots through the quiet sea. I had secured the mainsheet to the cleat. The tiller needed only slight pressure; and we all relaxed, eyes half-closed.

Suddenly Alexis shouted and jumped, knocking Gregory and his chair to the deck. Alexis clutched his ear and bellowed.

From his ear he pulled a centipede. He held the wriggling, many-legged creature in front of himself and stared at it while he massaged his ear with his free hand.

Gregory shouted, "Throw the son of a bitch overboard! Get rid of the fucker!"

Alexis put his face a bit closer to the creature, smiled at it and said softly, "Poor thing, it has a hundred legs to eat for. No wonder it's so hungry." He looked around and saw a matchbox. He picked it up, opened it, and put the centipede in the box. "Never fear, my little bug, I'll put a spot of bread in with you and land you when we get ashore."

"For Christ's sweet sake," said Gregory, "is that what you call love?"

"Yes, helping the centipede is love."

"And so," said Gregory, "you love that goddam bug enough to have him bite your ear and poison you?"

"No, I don't want the centipede to bite my ear and poison me. But neither will I hurt the centipede — because I love it. Just as I wouldn't have hurt you if you had come after me with your knife earlier. That's because I love you."

Alexis opened the match box and looked at the centipede. He closed the box and said, "Love isn't restricted. If a man loves his wife or his parents or children and nothing else, then he doesn't love at all. Can an ocean wet one fish and leave the others dry? Can I love you, Gregory, and kill a hungry centipede?"

Gregory didn't reply. He walked forward, caught my eye, wagged his head from side to side. He put his forefinger to his temple and moved his finger in a circular motion.

I looked at the chart and found a cove where in about three hours we could anchor for the night if I felt like it. It depended on the weather. If it continued as it was now, I might sail all night. I showed the spot on the chart to the other men. Alexis said that the area in which we now were is famous for its fish and suggested I try my luck. Gregory challenged him, asking how could he kill and eat a fish if he loved everything in the world.

"It makes me sad," said Alexis, "but it's a necessity. All living things must eat other living things to stay alive. That includes God."

"Bravo, big priest!" said Gregory. "Now you're getting the smarts."

I told them to mind the boat while I looked for fishing tackle.

WEDNESDAY, 31 MAY, 1967

few minutes after casting the spinner, I had a strike —
a strong one. I began reeling in.

"It's a big son of a bitch!" shouted Gregory. "Play it
like your life depends on it. It's you against Poseidon. Steal from his
flock!"

It took me almost an hour; and the fish was a whopper.

I was proud of having caught the big fish. I had handled the brute
perfectly; and had brought the 20-pounder in with tackle designed for
smaller fish. Gregory and Alexis had watched me the entire time,
sitting by the tiller, not saying a word. When the exhausted fish was
alongside, I gaffed it and brought it on board, completing the opera-
tion alone.

After I bashed its head and it lay still, I looked at the creature
glistening in the sun; and a feeling of superiority, of power, of skill
filled me with exultation. Gregory mentioned that we'd get some
good meals from the fish.

I turned to him and said, "Do you think I handled him well?"

He put his arm around me in the manner of a teacher encouraging a stupid student who'd tried hard. "George," he said, "obviously you're satisfied with your performance. You don't need my confirmation. Look at it this way: you wash your neck and you put on a clean shirt. Do you expect me to tell you that your neck and shirt are clean? Don't seek such foolishness to soothe your inner fears. The applause of others is like wind on the side of a mountain. It means nothing. One only craves it when one is afraid."

He paused, rubbed his nose, then handed me his knife. "Here, George, gut the fish. It's the privilege of the conqueror to cut out the balls and heart of the vanquished. But it's not his privilege to ask for praise."

I said, "If, through skill and bravery I saved your life, would you praise and thank me?"

"No," he said. "I'd neither praise nor thank you. If you got pleasure from my being alive, then you already would have received all the praise and thanks you deserve, and, of course, that's the only praise and thanks having real worth. If you didn't get pleasure from having me alive, then you should — in your hypothetical case — have permitted me to die."

I told him that perhaps he'd change his mind if such an event happened in the future.

Gregory grinned and jabbed me in the ribs with his elbow. "You're goddam proud of the way you caught that fish, aren't you?"

I told him I was.

"Well", he said, "look at it realistically. Maybe there's not so much to be proud of. It may be that that fish was unhappy and wanted to be caught and eaten by you. Would that spoil your fun? Perhaps the fish had a nagging mate and owed money to every loan shark in the Mediterranean. Maybe he wanted to die. Perhaps that's why he grabbed your hook?"

I asked him, if the fish wanted to die, then why did it fight so hard.

"Pride and fear," said Gregory. "Frightened people spend half their lives planning their own defeats. But they always want to adorn their defeat with the jewels of apparent bravery. They want defeat; but they wish to appear heroic and successful at it. Hardly any people who commit suicide have the courage to go into the mountains and starve to death in a cave where no one will ever find them. Hell no, they have to jump off the Brooklyn Bridge or splatter the bedroom with blood."

I asked Gregory why he thought the fish wanted to commit suicide.

He laughed, "Here, cut him open."

I did.

"See how fat he is. See how his gullet is bulging with food. He had no reason for grabbing anything else to eat, especially the bait on your hook."

I said that maybe the fish was a glutton.

"Gluttony is in itself a form of fear and suicide. Hurry now George. I'll start the stove and slice some onions and tomatoes. By that time you'll have the fish filleted."

THURSDAY, 1 JUNE 1967

AT SEA

ENROUTE HYDRA TO GYTHION

~~~~~~~~~~~~~~~~~~~~~~

At midnight, the wind veered about thirty degrees and decreased. At 0130, we had Maleas Light on our starboard beam, and I changed course to 283°. I estimated our speed at three knots and figured that we'd be in the approaches to Elaphonisos Channel in about three hours. At that time, we would sight Spathi Light bearing 280°, almost dead ahead. At about 0530, we'd be on the fringe of the area Constantine had warned us against — the area where at this time of the year there might be severe and sudden squalls.

I got Gregory up and told him to take the watch. I gave him all details and told him to awaken me if the weather changed even a little or when he sighted Spathi. He listened, grunting with impatience as if there were no need to give him such detailed instructions. I didn't want there to be any misunderstanding, so I repeated my orders. After he acknowledged them, I went below to get some sleep. I was fatigued and dozed off immediately despite the moaning of the priest who again was seasick.

About 0300, asleep in my bunk, I sensed an increase in *Varvaros'* rolling and pitching. But Gregory hadn't called me so I assumed that we might just have passed a big steamer or something like that. I drifted back into sleep even though Alexis, in his misery, was making a racket.

Sometime later I was tossed from my bunk by a great lurch of the boat, which was followed by a hell of a crashing sound. I thought it was a collision. I rushed topside. We had run into a sudden Elaphonisos Channel squall — the kind Constantine had predicted might happen. We apparently had just entered the storm, and I tried to figure out quickly how to run out of it. Conditions were worse than I'd expected. The waves were high. *Varvaros'* bow lifted and dropped in a noisy and sickening manner. Perhaps it was my imagination, but I believed I heard the fractured strake creaking and moving. The rain pelted hard, stinging and sounding like hail. We were heading 280°, about four miles off Cape Zovollo to starboard and Kithera about six miles to port. Gregory had lowered the sail. I raged. Why hadn't the son of a bitch called me? And now, when we could use another strong hand, the goddam priest was conked out in his bunk, helpless, puking, and moaning and groaning almost as loud as the storm.

Gregory stood by the tiller, his feet spread wide apart, holding the tiller with both hands. He shouted, "Go back to sleep! I'll handle this until daylight. Or until the storm's over."

I stared at him. He wore a yellow slicker top, a sou'wester rain hat, and bathing trunks.

He shouted, "Goddamit, go back to bed! This is no time for amateurs."

Over the noise of the storm, I heard the terrible sound of the fractured strake working. *Varvaros* was screaming with pain.

"Gregory! Take her about — downwind!"

"I told you to get the hell out of here. I know how to sail better than you do!"

I made my way to the cockpit and said, "Gregory, I'll take over."

"I told you, you stupid son of a bitch, to go below. We're in a squall and you don't know shit from beans about sailing."

"This is my boat," I said, pushing him away from the tiller.

He resisted me, taking his hands from the tiller to shove me away. The tiller swung to starboard. *Varvaros* began to move abruptly to port. This threw Gregory and me against each other. We began grappling for the tiller. Gregory got behind me, grabbed me by the collar, pulled me away, shouting, "Get the hell out of here, you stupid bastard."

I twisted to get away from him and, perhaps accidentally, struck him hard in the mouth with my hand. Gregory's hold on my collar loosened, and as I twisted again and the ship lurched, we collided hard. Gregory lost his balance, tottered, desperately reached out to grab something. But there was nothing to grab, and he fell backward — overboard into the ocean and the darkness.

For a moment I froze as it flashed through my mind that from the sequence of the struggle it would appear to Gregory that I had pushed him overboard. If I had a life preserver or a life jacket to throw over, he could stay afloat all night if need be or until the storm passed over us. Constantine had said they are like small hurricanes and move on quickly.

In that instant the wind seemed to increase; and I knew that to rescue Gregory, I'd have to take the boat well up into the wind — while we still could do it — and drift down on him. If the wind got worse and we drifted downwind and past him, I'd probably not be able to find him.

It took what seemed to be forever to start the old engine. I threw the throttle to full ahead. I pushed the tiller over, and *Varvaros* slowly headed into the wind — but very, very slowly. *Varvaros* moved slowly — I estimated about one knot at most. Astern of us about 20 or 30 feet, I saw a pip of yellow. *Varvaros* now was into the wind, and I took a quick bearing on the vanishing yellow pip. I calculated that if we were making good one knot, in about five minutes we'd move into the wind anywhere from between 250 and 500 feet, and I could turn *Varvaros* around and drift into the bearing where I hoped Gregory was

(As I write this about eight hours after it happened, my description makes me appear cool and competent. But I was frightened and desperate. I was frightened lest Gregory drown — and I felt the fault was mine.)

I made sure the engine was on full speed ahead. Still we didn't seem to be moving — or, at least, not much; so I decided to stay on this course a few more minutes. I shouted for Alexis, hoping he could come up and help.

Every minute seemed a century, and even though I kept looking for Gregory and watching the boat, my mind wandered.

I recalled the conversation Gregory and I had had just after I'd caught the fish. He said he'd not thank me if I saved his life. Well, here he was overboard and needed saving. He had said — with irritating arrogance — that the only reason for me to save his life would be if his being alive gave me satisfaction and pleasure.

Those few minutes were a terrible emotional crisis for me. I asked myself, Should I let him drown? I hated that son-of-a-bitch; he'd forced his way aboard *Varvaros* and had tried to take command of both *Varvaros* and me.

I had to decide if I should turn *Varvaros* then and drift down on him, or at least to where I thought he was. I decided to get further into the wind.

Well, I thought, the bastard has his own snail's shell now — a big one — the whole Aegean Sea — with the nearest beach about 4 miles away!

The wind shifted suddenly. We would have to come more to the left if we were to drift down on Gregory. I put the tiller over.

I remembered how he had outthought me when I was repairing

the boat; and how he had outsmarted me in conversation and also that he could dance Greek dances and I couldn't. Even within the last few days he'd worked hard to frustrate and annoy me and do things I didn't want to do. I'd bought *Varvaros* to simplify my life, to find freedom; and if it hadn't been for that parasite Gregory I'd be sailing alone — even if I didn't know how, and even if the rudder had dropped off and the engine conked out and even if I'd wrecked the boat on the rocks.

I kept desperately looking for Gregory and trying to judge whether or not I was putting *Varvaros* in the right position. Gregory was astern someplace — floundering, maybe drowning. I was in charge. Did that mean I was free? Does freedom mean that one must always be alone and always in complete control?

However, even as I was thinking these things, I had pushed the tiller over and had brought *Varvaros* around. I eased the throttle and we began drifting downwind toward the spot where I estimated that Gregory should be.

I switched on the searchlight — and it worked well. I thought, when Gregory found what was wrong with the searchlight, perhaps he made it possible for him to extend his life by a hell of a long time. It would be impossible to find him without the light.

At that moment Alexis staggered up on deck. He fell on deck — sprawled out — his arms hanging over the side — and he threw up, again and again, retching and groaning. He tried to put his head over the side as he continued to throw up, spasming and groaning. Jesus, I thought, I don't want him over the side too. I left the tiller for a moment, grabbed Alexis' feet and dragged him amidships and shouted, "Get below! Get below!" *Varvaros* began to swing into the wind. I left Alexis and went back to the tiller. I still hadn't decided how to rescue Gregory, and as we drifted slowly downwind, I knew if I didn't save him, it'd be the same as murdering him. Yet if he drowned, no one would know the circumstances. It would be an accident in a storm. There were no witnesses. I'd not be blamed.

The freak rain squall suddenly went by us, as they do in Greek waters. The thunderclouds had passed over us. We were out of the vortex even though the waves still were high and there was a slight rain. However the wind went down and the visibility began to improve. It was like staggering from one world into another. About 50 feet ahead, I saw Gregory bobbing up and down. He had removed the yellow slicker top. He was floating on his back and waving at me with one arm.

With the wind down, the noise now was only the loud slapping of the waves, the chug, chug of the engine, and Alexis' puking and groaning. I put the engine into neutral, and we began to drift closer to Gregory. I put over the rope ladder used for climbing aboard from the dinghy.

Gregory now was treading water. He grinned and shouted, "See, you want me to live! Saving me gives you pleasure!"

"Shut up and grab the rope ladder, you bastard!"

We drifted closer.

Gregory was still grinning. "Georgie," he shouted, "it would've been easy to let me go — the perfect crime — but you're a coward! You know I might've made it to the beach or could have stayed afloat until daylight and then somebody else would have picked me up . . ."

We were almost down on him now, and in about thirty seconds he could have grabbed the rope ladder.

He continued, "And then I'd tell everybody you had left me out here and you're a murderer. That scared the shit out of you, didn't it, Georgie boy?"

Gregory started swimming toward the rope ladder. I pushed the throttle ahead, steered away from him and shouted back, "Swim the four miles to the beach, you bastard, if that's what you want. Make your own decision."

Gregory looked startled.

"Tread water all night, you fucker, if that's what you want."

He continued swimming toward us even as we moved away.

I shouted, "If you want to be picked up, then ask for it! You'll stay out there until you beg me."

Alexis, even with his seasickness and misery, caught on to what was happening. Lying on the deck, partially in his own muck, he turned his head and roared, "Save him! For God's sake save him!"

I didn't answer.

Alexis pulled his big hulk to his knees and started crawling toward me — his face moving like a maniac's, his hands reaching out toward me like two great grapnels.

"Get back, Alexis! Stay away! You can help more by staying away!"

Alexis kept coming, his grappling-hook hands waving and reaching out while he shouted, "Save him! For God's sake save him!"

He was only about two feet from me and I thought Jesus, if he gets his hands on me the three of us'll be overboard. He started to stand up. I kicked out to push him away — I didn't dare take my hands from the tiller. At that moment he bent over, turned his face to puke again — and my kick landed on the side of his head. Alexis flopped over and lay still.

Gregory, still was grinning and swam with strong strokes toward the boat. I pushed the throttle full ahead and moved the boat away. Gregory now swam with a burst of speed, obviously determined to catch hold of the rope ladder and pull himself up regardless of anything I'd said.

I kept the boat away from him.

I shouted, "Good-bye, Gregory," and moved the boat away.

Gregory stopped grinning. He tread high in the water and beckoned me frantically, calling, "Please! Please!"

I backed *Varvaros* a little and said to him, "If you want to come aboard, beg for it!"

I put the engine into neutral and waited. Gregory began talking, not shouting as before. What he said was barely audible, but I watched his lips and knew what he was saying: "Please, George, I don't want to die. Please, George, save me."

I waved for him to swim over. He started — and I saw he was more tired than I had expected. He swam with slow, weak strokes. He grabbed the rope ladder hanging over the side — but couldn't pull himself up.

"Help me, George, I can't make it."

"Then rest a while. I don't trust you!"

He hung there for a few minutes and then slowly, laboriously, pulled himself aboard *Varvaros*. When he got on deck he just lay there — right next to Alexis. I reached under Gregory's arms, dragged him across the deck and down the ladder into the cabin. He was still inert; he began moaning. He wasn't coughing so I knew he hadn't swallowed or breathed in much water. He was exhausted and beaten.

Varvaros began turning and rolling. I rushed topside and turned her back into the wind. Alexis still was out. I held *Varvaros* on course for about twenty minutes — and during that time, the sea calmed noticeably. By now Alexis was sitting up, rubbing the side of his head.

I went back below. Gregory was in his bunk. I poured a great slug of whiskey, handed it to him.

He sipped it slowly, carefully — as if it were the Cup of Life. When he had finished, he said in a weak voice, "George, I told you that you were too much of a coward to let me drown. That *was* true — yesterday — but it's not true anymore. There are rules for cowards — and there are other rules for those who are not cowards."

I said nothing.

"George, look at me," he said.

I looked at him directly. He spoke slowly, without smiling.

"George, I thank you for saving my life."

I was about to tell him, "You're welcome," but I didn't. Other words came from my mouth, words that I hadn't planned to say. Somehow they hadn't come from my brain. What came from my mouth, instead, was, "There's no need to thank me, Gregory. The fact is I saved my own life — not yours."

"I'm grateful, George. One doesn't know who has courage and who is a coward until one finds oneself playing hopscotch with death. I learned that I'm a coward."

He began to sob.

Alexis came below, hunched over, still rubbing the side of his head. He climbed into his bunk, gave a dry heave, pulled the blanket over his head, and lay still.

I went topside. The sea had calmed. The wind had decreased to about ten knots. The canvas was wet and I had a hard time hoisting sail alone, but I managed it. I shut off the engine and steadied *Varvaros* on course. Cape Spathi Light was clearly visible at 260°, as were the mountains of Kithera to port. It was beginning to get light. The Gulf of Lakonikos lay straight ahead about twelve miles. We'd be in Gythion by 1400.

THURSDAY, 1 JUNE 1967

AT SEA

ENROUTE HYDRA TO GYTHION

〜〜〜〜〜〜〜〜〜〜

The sun is up. The wind is steady. I am depleted physically and psychically; yet I feel lightheaded and filled with a warmth that I cannot think of any word for except love. I think of Gregory and Alexis with compassion and I am wondering when they'll be up and what I can do for them. I'll awaken them in about an hour. I wonder how they'll be and how I will respond.

As I write this, Gregory has just come up, carrying a bucket and a swab. He was smiling — a smile good and deep. He seemed pleased to see me; and he came to me, touched his cheeks to mine. "Good morning," he said, "we're cleaning up the mess below and we'll make breakfast soon. You must be dead tired."

He scooped up a bucket of water and went below. I left the tiller and began making breakfast.

We ate our breakfast with Gregory doing most of the talking at first. He told in detail how I had done a great job of seamanship. I didn't know how to respond, so I changed the subject and told them about the Athos book and my schedule for writing it. I told them that while *Varvaros* was being repaired, I'd be in Athens researching the lives of twelve saints. And then I'd sail *Varvaros* to Athos and write about them, anchoring near the monasteries where they had lived.

When Alexis heard the names of the saints, he recalled that almost all of them had fasted at the start of their monkhoods. He said, "Forty days of fasting in the wilderness — just as Jesus did. I did it once for nineteen days and in my arrogance thought I had learned everything. Now I'll start all over when I return to Athos. It's a wonderful, joyful experience, but one must be patient. One's soul floats up like the rising sun, and every minute is like an illuminated lifetime. Yes, I'll fast for forty days the next time."

Having said that, Alexis began roaring with laughter, deep bellows starting at his heels. Then he said, "But my fasting hasn't started yet — and it won't as long as Captain Giorghos is doing the cooking."

With that he dipped bread into the Spanish omelet sauce, stuffed it in his mouth, and washed it down with wine. "We mustn't forget," he said, "when we eat well — especially good food that has been cooked with love — it's a glorious way of worshipping God."

He grinned, then took the pan and scooped what was left of the omelet onto his plate.

During breakfast, Alexis (the left side of his face is black, blue, and swollen) said, "Last night I was so sick I thought I'd die. Yes, I thought I'd die. When one is near death, it's like dreaming; and as I lay on the deck with my intestines coming out of my mouth, I dreamed — well, it was more than a dream, and yet it was a dream — that Captain Giorghos was overboard and Gregory was trying to save him, but that Gregory didn't know how. I was too weak to do anything but shout. I don't even know what I shouted. Then I felt I had to help and I tried to get up."

Alexis stopped talking because he choked up with emotion. He looked for a handkerchief to blow his nose; and he couldn't find one, so he wiped his nose and his eyes on his sleeve.

"Then God told me not to move. God said that what was happening was good. It was something that had to happen for God's sake. Yes, for God's own sake. And I tell you, God's voice thundered with *kyros.** God told me to stay away. But I didn't want Captain Giorghos to drown, so I tried to move and help. And, God struck me — oh, what a blow, like a bolt of lightning from the Old Testament. That's all I remember. But, oh, the *kyros* in that voice! Look at my face. Look at that mark! Now I know what to do. I'll go back to the monastery and learn how to listen with purity."

**Kyros:* Greek for "with authority."

THURSDAY, 1 JUNE 1967

GYTHION

~~~~~~~~~~~~~~~~~~

W e arrived at the Skala Yannakatis at 1440. As I was about to jump on to the dock at the small shipyard, Alexis came on deck, carrying his suitcase. He said in a little while he'd depart and go to Sparta — as soon as I knew when *Varvaros'* repairs would be completed. I nodded and went ashore. Near the end of the dock I saw a man mending a nylon fishnet. He was fat, dark, and old. He had big hands with fishhook scars, and when the old man looked up I saw that his eyes had bumps on the corneas and there were deep lines running from his eyes to his temples — the trademarks of mariners who have squinted into the sun too much. I asked him if he could direct me to Mr. Yannakatis. He continued mending the net and said, "I'm Yannakatis."

I pointed my thumb toward *Varvaros* and told him I was Adamson. Yannakatis stood up, beckoned me to follow him. He took me to his house about a hundred yards inland. Inside he brought me jam, cookies, and coffee.

"So you had a collision and broke a strake?"

He told me that Constantine had telephoned and that he would be here tomorrow to help work on the boat. He wasn't being paid — he *wanted* to work on the boat. Then Yannakatis asked if I'd be staying here. I told him no.

He said he didn't know exactly how much he'd have to do on the boat, but that if I were back in three weeks, everything would be completed. He got up and said he'd look at the damage.

When we got to the end of the dock, the old man, who was at least seventy, nimbly leaped aboard *Varvaros* and without a word went below. Alexis came forward from the fantail and asked me how long it would be, and I told him three weeks. He hugged me and said he'd see me in three weeks; or, if his friends were not in Sparta, he'd look me up in Athos in about a month. Picking up his suitcase, he walked ashore.

Gregory wasn't topside. I looked for him below. He wasn't there either. Neither was his knapsack. I ran after Alexis and asked where Gregory was. "While you were in Yannakatis' house," he said, "Gregory put on his knapsack and went ashore. He just waved good-bye and left."

When I got back to the boat, I went below. Yannakatis was thumping the hull. "Yes," he said, "it sounds fractured. But I won't know how badly until I get into it. But it'll be done within three weeks. You'll be back then for sure?"

"Yes, for sure."

"Where can I reach you?"

I gave him Agios' name, address, and telephone number; and asked Yannakatis for an estimate. He said about 18,000 drachmas — about $600. I asked if he wanted a deposit. He laughed and said no — Constantine was deposit enough.

THURSDAY, 1 JUNE 1967
ENROUTE GYTHION TO MISTRA

~~~~~~~~~~~~~~~~~~~~

I'm on a bus to Athens via Mistra (about 1 1/4 hours from Gythion). Mistra is a Byzantine city with many old churches and convents. They have archives that might be rich in anecdotes. I'll stay there for a day. Very difficult writing on this bumpy bus. The Greeks on either side of me are trying to read what I'm writing. I can hardly read it myself. Besides, it is in English. I feel good — I guess "stable" is the word. I have what seems to be a new energy in me — a gentle energy. I've been thinking about this. In my book *The Strange Energies*, I gave evidence concerning: (1) people who drain energies from others; and (2) people who emanate negative energies that confuse and contaminate others. Hitler and Senator Joseph McCarthy come to mind.

It hadn't occurred to me that if there are energy parasites and spewers of negative energies — then it's possible that there also are givers of physical vigor and donors of positive energy. I am astonished at my oversight. Is it possible that this is what saints, holy people, and healers are all about?

We can easily — with electronic instruments — measure the energy field surrounding the human body; and I've done it often. But my experiments largely concerned the depletion of human energies by others, not the increasing. I guess I was too hepped on witch theory to think about anything else. Rudi von Urban told me that the University of Upsala has sophisticated equipment for measuring the human energy field that surrounds our bodies. Perhaps I can stop at Upsala on the way home after I've finished the book.

God, I don't see how, in my research, I neglected the phenomenon of transferring positive energy and concentrated on the negative. It tells a lot about me!

We're now entering Sparta. Mistra is only fifteen minutes away.

FRIDAY, 2 JUNE 1967
ENROUTE MISTRA TO ATHENS

~~~~~~~~~~~~~~~~~~~~~~~~~~~~

L ast night an old nun — a church historian for convents — advised me to look up a monk named Electros of Caracallou Monastery, now working at the Athens Museum. He's been doing research on saints and relics for thirty years. He's trained as an anthropologist and has been carbon testing relics to ascertain their ages.

Tonight I'll check into the King George, and at dinner I'll give Agios the forty-page outline. I've done a sample chapter on St. Gregory and a half a page or so on each of the other saints. I know the history of the mountain inside out; and my book on it probably is *the* definitive one on the subject. The new book will be intimate biographies, full of anecdotes, facts, alleged miracles. I must look at the tons of manuscripts and relics scattered throughout various monasteries on Athos. For access and assistance I am dependent upon the goodwill and approval of the church. They admire my last book (it's used as a textbook in church schools); and now I must persuade them that the humanizing of the saints — showing that they started out as ordinary human beings and thus are examples we can all follow if we are willing to pay the price — is of benefit to the church. Agios will show them the outline.

I wonder if there'll be mail for me in Athens. I hope not. The only possible mail would be bills. Sheila's last letter mentioned the good time we had in Crete eleven years ago. We did have a good time there. Sheila and I always had a wonderful time when we were traveling. But when at home — oh!

In a few weeks — after my research in Athens is completed — I'll pick up *Varvaros*, sail her to Daphne harbor, and then plunge into my writing. Once I begin, there will be neither time nor energy for anyone or anything else. Not even for maintaining this journal.

Once I start the actual writing, I must concentrate on it and forget about myself. I must become the twelve saints, the typewriter, the letters on the pages.

FRIDAY, 2 JUNE 1967
ATHENS

~~~~~~~~~~~~~~~~~~~~

The suite that Agios had laid on for me here at the King George Hotel is like a gold and silk sybaritic dream. All my life I've gotten much pleasure from the razzle-dazzle with which publishers treat their authors. It was part of the trappings of literary success. But, somehow, now, after the simplicity of Lesvos and the basics of *Varvaros,* this all seems like sitting down to a ten-course meal when all I have an appetite for is an apple and a piece of cheese. Perhaps the fact that I've lost twelve pounds and am having a sense of self-discipline from daily exercising and can feel the sap of vitality rising in me is influencing my tastes? Regardless, I'm grateful to Agios for his generosity and thoughtfulness.

There was a letter from Kitty* waiting for me:

Dear George,

Thank you very much for the cool Greek bracelet you sent me for my birthday. It's beautiful and all the girls at school love it and say how

*Katherine, Sheila's fifteen-year-old daughter.

lucky I am to have a stepfather who sends presents even after he's divorced from my mother. I want you to know that I love you and Meg* loves you and I think that Ma still loves you. Ma has gone back to school at night and is studying philosophy and she also has a job in the beauty department at Elizabeth Arden. She starts next Monday. I have a job baby sitting and now I have to go because I hear the baby crying and I hate to change diapers but this is about the only way a teenager can make bread.

Love,
Kitty

Agios stopped over to see if everything was alright and to pick up the outline of the manuscript. He was pleased with how I looked but said we should wait a month or two more before meeting the press. "We want to knock them dead," he said. He's spending the evening with several bishops, reading and discussing the outline. "If we're publishing a book about saints, it's wise to work hand in glove with the church. If they like it we have a built-in distribution organization."

Agios is coming in the morning for breakfast.

*Margaret, Sheila's twelve-year-old daughter.

SATURDAY, 3 JUNE 1967
ATHENS

~~~~~~~~~~~~~~~~~

Agios and two bishops called on me early this morning. They're wild about the outline. Agios hurried off a few minutes later but the bishops stayed for breakfast. They said the church will give me assistance as needed.

When would I go to Athos to begin the book?

What were my plans?

I told them I'd sail *Varvaros* to Daphne within two or three weeks and would use *Varvaros* as a floating office. That would allow me to bring a typewriter, reference books, cameras, and so forth to various monastery ports in Athos without the burden of lugging several hundred pounds of gear from monastery to monastery; and it would give me a place where I could write in private.

They thought this a good idea, but warned me that the seas sometimes are rough at this time of year and I should get a pilot who knows the area. How long would I be at Athos? How long will it take to write the book? And then what?

I told them I'd be in Athos about three months and would complete the book while there. Then I'd give the manuscript to Agios; I had requested Agios to submit it to the church for checking for factual, spiritual, or attitudinal errors that I might make; and while the church and Agios were reading manuscript, I would go back to Athos for personal reasons. I wanted to stay in a skete for six weeks alone — to fast, pray, meditate. The bishops both smiled. One said, "So, you've heard the Holy Mother?" (I suppose he was referring to a chapter in my last Athos book that tells the legend of how the Mother of God chose Athos as her garden.) I nodded. They nodded back and said they were certain the Council at Karyai would give permission.

RESEARCHING IN ATHENS

~~~~~~~~~~~~~~~~~~~~

The various archives here in Athens have vast stores of material. There are thirteen centuries of information about people who lived on Athos. The Greek librarians have done a wonderful job; and everyone is pleasant and helpful. I found Electros at the museum; and he showed me the files that list the most important documents on Mount Athos, monastery by monastery. This is my key.

After *Varvaros'* primitive vitality, I find it difficult to be emotionally comfortable in King George's luxury. And a vast suite at that! I should have someone here with me. There are two double beds and a sitting room.

I have cabled Maria, inviting her.

Maria telephoned from Mythymna refusing my invitation to stay with me at the King George, but saying she'd like to see me when the book's completed. Constantine telephoned from Gythion asking if he could come to Athens and see me about an important matter that he didn't want to discuss over the phone. Yes, of course. I hope they haven't found more serious damage in *Varvaros*.

TUESDAY, 13 JUNE 1967

ATHENS

~~~~~~~~~~~~~~~~~

The first thing Constantine said after coming up was that I must be a millionaire to live in this place. I explained that the bill was being paid by my publisher and, frankly, I didn't even have enough money to pay my ex-wife's divorce money.

Then he came to the urgent reason for his visit. He missed *Varvaros* and wanted to buy her back at my convenience.

"Captain," he said, "here's my proposition. I know you've put a lot of work into her and she's a better boat now than when you bought her. Okay. But there's the bill at Yannakatis. I'll pay Yannakatis and give you U.S. two thousand eight hundred."

I told him I needed *Varvaros* for three months more or less — and I explained my plan at Athos.

"What will you do with *Varvaros* after that?"

I told him I hadn't thought about that.

"Okay," he said, "let's talk about it. Let me tell you, you'll need a pilot and boatkeeper at Athos. The occasional storms at this time of year are rough. Suppose I do that for you. I'll pilot her wherever

you need her and look after her while you're working at the monasteries. At the end of three or four months you sell her back to me —
and I'll give you U.S. two thousand."

I thought for a while. This was a generous proposition that would
be good for me — but there was one hitch. There might be rewriting
to do. I might have to go back to Athos for more work. I said to
Constantine, "Let's agree on it — but if I need *Varvaros* for more
than three and a half months, then I'll pay you U.S. four hundred
a month to run the boat; and when I'm through with my tour and
return to America, I'll sell you the boat for U.S. two thousand."

He beamed, put his hand out and said, "You're more Greek than
American."

We shook hands on the deal.

He asked me if I'd made arrangements for an entry permit to
Athos. Yes, I had. He asked could I arrange one for him also? Yes,
I'd take care of it.

He started for the door, smiling, said, "But remember, even when
I look after *Varvaros*, you're still the captain."

"Why do you want *Varvaros* back?" I asked.

He said, "When I saw you looking at *Varvaros* several months ago,
I *knew* you had to have her; and when you saw her, *you* knew you
had to have her. The Fates spoke to both of us. Soon you won't need
her any more. The Fates now have spoken again, and they say that
it's time for *Varvaros* to come back home to me. You're a Greek in
your heart and you know that what I'm saying is true."

SATURDAY, 17 JUNE 1967

ATHENS

~~~~~~~~~~~~~~~~~~~~~~

My research in Athens is completed — I'm a week ahead of schedule. Constantine telephoned that *Varvaros* will be ready to sail in two days. Constantine and Yannakatis will bring the boat to Passalimani, where I'll embark on Wednesday. Yannakatis wants to make a pilgrimage to Athos and has asked if he can ride up with us. Of course, but would he leave a note at his place telling where *Varvaros* is? Alexis may come back and look for her.

In four days I'll be in Athos. Very soon my writing will begin, and already I feel the inner trembling and fright that always afflicts me at this stage. For me the task requires all my energy and all my time. There's nothing left over for anybody or anything else. Perhaps that's why I'm so bloody hard to live with?

This is the last entry in my journal until the book is completed — about three months. Until then, journal, sleep well.

PUBLISHER'S NOTE: *George made no entries in his journal during the three months he was writing his book on Mount Athos. The only firsthand information we have concerning that period is in a letter that I, Agios Papandillis, received 20 August 1967.*

Dear Agios,

The book will be completed on schedule, but at this moment I am frustrated on one point. What was the catalyst of the saints' spiritual births? There's a vital iota missing — something that is beyond my frame of experience. As a journalist, I cannot report or describe the "spiritual birth."

Almost all of the saints about whom I'm writing had one thing in common in their early careers. Each "went into the wilderness for forty days and fasted" — just as Jesus did (and also Moses, Buddha, and holy men and women in almost all major religions). As hard as I explore, I cannot find out what happened *during* their forty days of fasting — even though we have information about which cave, which mountain, or which hidden canyon they chose as their "wilderness."

There are no diaries, no accounts, not even myths or legends of what happened *during* those forty days. To my knowledge, no one knows about their actual adventures. There are many detailed accounts of how they changed during the forty days, what they looked like and how they acted upon returning to their social communities, but *not of what happened.* "His face shown with Divine radiance." "He had been arrogant and abrupt, but when he came back to the monastery he was gentle and humble." Over and over, we hear or read of their profound changes, their starts on the way to sainthood, the shining of the Holy Spirit from them — but *nothing about the process.*

This information is not absolutely necessary for the book, but my personal curiosity is clawing at me. The "forty days of fasting in the wilderness" appears to be a key in the spiritual development of many of the world's great religious figures. We know the end result, but not its substance. I've asked two bishops up here and they shrugged.

I also have been saddened by a dismal observation. Even though the monasteries are glories of architecture, religious art, chronicles, and artifacts of measureless value, the monasteries currently are infirm. The vigors that created these glories have departed. Most of the monasteries are peopled by a handful of old, tired monks. Monasteries that formerly had three or four thousand spiritual workers now have only thirty of forty caretakers. This suggests that Jesus and Ecclesiastes were right after all. The creation of great materials — including religious treasures and dogma — is a vanity that Time ultimately will destroy — and that only the spirit principle lasts. In the last millenium and a half, much of the monks' energies has been spent in rebuilding the monasteries and treasures that were sacked, burned, stolen by pirates, vandals, or western Christians; or were destroyed by natural calamities. Only the memories of the saints, and spiritual principles, appear to live on and endure regardless of events and Time.

The precious, vigorous spirit still exists with a few individuals in Athos, but most (not all) of those whom I've met live alone or in small groups in isolated sketes. I met three wonderfully spiritual monks in a St. Anne's skete. They were artists who painted icons for the church to sell. The three had the Radiance — their buoyant spirit lifted me the moment I entered their small house, and it continues to renew me whenever I recall them. They told me that there were four of them, "but Stamatis isn't here now." I asked where Stamatis was, and they replied, "He's fasting on the mountain." For how long? "For forty days, like Jesus."

I asked what happened during the forty days. The three monks laughed, "One gets very skinny — here, like this," said one of them, pointing to an icon they had painted of Jesus fasting in the wilderness. It was a skin and bones Jesus who glowed with the Radiance.

Again I asked what happened during the forty days. One monk said, "One learns that God, *Diavolos*, and Thee are all the same." Another said, "It is inexpressible." The third said, "In Revelation, it is said, 'Behold, I stand at the door and knock; if anyone opens the door, I will come in.' When one is fasting in the wilderness, there is no clatter of pots and pans to drown out His soft knock."

I kept pressing them for a description of the forty days' experience. One monk said, "The *synergeia* and the deification are inexpressible." The others nodded, then, smiling, steered me to the dinner table — a slab of stone on two sawhorses — beans, tomatoes, radikia, and wine. And they asked me questions about what was happening in the rest of the world.

That's the closest I've gotten to the vital information — and I'm still light years away.

Writing this book is physically wearying. My eyes hurt from translating holy documents in bad light. My larynx is sore from asking questions. I'm constantly yawning from lack of sleep. I go to the monasteries at dawn and get back to *Varvaros* late at night — and then must write for hours about what I've learned during the long day. My back and thighs are blotched with what I'm certain are vermin bites. Never mind all that, my energies are full and strong and I am doing what I love, on a subject I love. And even though the monasteries at the moment are anachronisms, the Holy Mountain itself pulses with inspiring life. Here one perceives the forces that (under both ancient pagan and then Christian rule) have molded and sustained the grandeur of Hellas; and I predict that the monasteries in the future again will come alive and will teem with thousands of spiritually energetic monks. The flowing strength of Athos plus world conditions makes this inevitable.

I will be back in Athens the day I promised — and will bring the completed manuscript. Rest your eyes and get a good sleep the evening before I arrive. And, old friend, plan a sybaritic meal. Eating beans, radikia, and bread three meals a day at the monasteries makes me hunger for your Epicurean table.

Love,
Giorghos

WEDNESDAY, 13 SEPTEMBER 1967
BACK AGAIN IN PASSALIMANI HARBOR

~~~~~~~~~~~~~~~~~~~~~~~~~~~~~~~~~

H *ello, Journal, I'm back.*

Two days ago at dawn, *Varvaros*, Constantine, the completed manuscript, and I departed Daphne. We arrived in Passalimani at ten this morning. I had lunch with Agios and delivered the book. He promised to read it immediately; and we will meet again tomorrow.

I am living aboard *Varvaros*, getting pleasure from doing nothing. No more interviewing, no more examining relics, no more checking out anecdotes, no more translating thousand-year-old scrolls, no more staying up half the night typing and retyping. Nothing — that's what I'm doing. But I'm impatient to get Agios' opinion on whether the book needs revision or if it's sufficient as is.

If I have to revise manuscript, then we will sail *Varvaros* back to Athos and go back to work.

If the book stands as is, *Varvaros* and I will part. Constantine will sail *Varvaros* to Crete to visit his family, and I will make my way back to Athos. This time I'm going to the Holy Mountain for myself —

for my inner personal exploration. I will "go into the wilderness and fast for forty days." I'm frightened. Nevertheless I've made preliminary arrangements with the council at Karyai and the abbot at St. Anne's. I requested permission to fast for forty days in the same cave where Anthimus supposedly fasted in 1726. I haven't been in it (the monk-guide — when I was there as a writer — said only those with religious missions are allowed to enter), but the location is in spectacular wilderness. It is on the southwest tip of the peninsula in the Karoulia area. The cave is at the top of a cliff that drops straight down (what seems to be about a thousand feet) into the sea. It is a wild spot, very difficult to reach. Why did I choose the Anthimus cave? Why make the task so hard? I don't know. Perhaps I'm trying to prove to myself that I'm a hero? Perhaps because Anthimus did his best writing in that lonely, dark, harsh cave?

Constantine just told me there's a Charlie Chaplin movie in town and suggested we eat out and see it. What a good idea! I relish a change from monastery beans and tomatoes, and a belly laugh will nourish my soul.

WEDNESDAY, 13 SEPTEMBER 1967
PASSALIMANI HARBOR

~~~~~~~~~~~~~~~~~~~~~~~~~~~~~~~~~~

T he messenger from Agios' office delivered a letter from
Sheila. It was a fat letter in a large brown envelope. I
received it with reluctance, with dread. It had to be a
bunch of old bills she wanted me to pay. For a moment I imagined
Ziggy standing by the gangplank, shaking her head and saying,
"Maybe you've painted your women bad when they may have been
very good."

I opened the fat envelope. There were no bills. It was a long
handwritten letter.

Dear George,

Mimi telephoned this morning. She says she's going blind, has had a
breast removed (cancer), and believes she will die soon. She desperately
wants to see you, her son, before she dies, and she placed great emphasis
on the "my son" part. She's despondent and lonely. Her birthday's on
the twenty-sixth, and she pathetically begged me, "my son's wife" (she
doesn't seem to remember that we've been divorced), to be with her on

her birthday. If I can get two days off I'll go, even though I hardly know her. The only time I met her was at Tom's wedding, and you got upset because of my resemblance to her, and as you may recall you were in a bad mood for days after that. Anyway, I'll try to cheer her up and I will explain to her that you're incommunicado someplace in the wilds of Greece.

If I can get to Mimi's a day early, I'll be spending *my* birthday with her. My forty-third. Mimi's twenty-eight years plus one day older than I am.

A new subject: I thought it might interest you to know that I've gone back to school. I'm at Columbia night school twice a week studying philosophy. George, I remember with sadness how I used to resent your urging me to go back to school. I felt you were trying to tell me that you were smarter and more intelligent than I was. I hated you when as a birthday present you gave me the tuition money for a semester of college, and I remember how furious you were when I spent the money on clothes. Good Lord! What we used to do to each other! Well, dear ex-husband, I'm now studying philosophy, and we're now into your favorite philosopher, Heraclitus. Here's how I summed him up for class the other night: "Knowledge consists in comprehending the all-pervading harmony. Virtue consists in subordination of the individual to the laws of harmony. It is only here that true freedom is found. Hot and cold, good and evil, night and day, etc. are the same in the sense that they are inseparable halves of one and the same thing."

I have a full-time job at Elizabeth Arden, where I teach women how to camouflage themselves and pretend they're beautiful. Wonderful pay, but now that I've been at school for several months the very word "cosmetics" gives me the shivers. Except when I'm working, I don't use makeup any more. I recall also with sadness how annoyed I was with you when you told me I was prettier without makeup and how I interpreted this as your trying to show that your taste was superior to mine.

The girls and I have become "health nuts." No sugar, coffee, alcohol, and very little meat. Fish and fowl moderately. Whole grains. Plenty of exercise. And can you believe it, George, I've put on weight!

Our divorce was traumatic for both of us, but in some ways it has been a blessing. We're no longer trying to murder each other and compete over every darn issue. You have started doing again that which you love most, which is writing. I hope to God it's going well for you. I, as a result of studying philosophy, am learning for the first time what it means to be alive. Heraclitus said there must be painful shocks before there is upward progress. I'm not certain, but I seem to remember your telling me that once.

God bless,
Sheila.

I swallowed a few times after reading what is the best letter I ever received from Sheila. I airmailed her a birthday present: the bronze Athena door knocker that I'd found in Hydra. It took me all day to get customs clearance to send an antique out of the country. I sent a note saying that Athena was not only the goddess of wisdom but also the goddess of students who went to night school and, incidentally, was the goddess most admired and worshipped by Heraclitus.

Oh, happy Thursday!

14 SEPTEMBER 1967

~~~~~~~~~~~~

Agios says the book is the best I've ever done, that it is superb and needs almost no changes. He has shown it to the church elders. They are enthusiastic and tentatively have ordered 2,000 copies to send out on some celebration that takes place next year. The church suggested the book be titled *The Soul of Greece.* I told Agios I'd leave the title decision to him.

Now I can settle with Constantine about *Varvaros* and return to Athos to pry into and recreate myself. I'll leave my gear and boxes of reference material with Agios.

THURSDAY, 14 SEPTEMBER 1967
ENROUTE PASSALIMANI TO ATHENS

~~~~~~

J ust before Constantine rowed me ashore, I took off my captain's hat and put it on his head, kissed his hand, and thanked him for all he'd done for me. He put the cap back on my head and said, "Captain Giorgho, *Varvaros* will be with you whenever you need her. Your inner strangers — now your friends, I hope — someday may want to go for another cruise with you. When that happens, just put on your captain's hat, and whoosh — *Varvaros* will come to you."

We embraced emotionally and I climbed into the dinghy.

When I got ashore, we loaded my gear into the waiting taxi. I saluted Constantine. I saluted *Varvaros*. Then pulling my captain's cap firmly on my head, I quickly got into the taxi and drove off. I couldn't bear to look back.

FRIDAY, 15 SEPTEMBER 1967
ENROUTE ATHENS TO OURANOPOLIS

~~~~~~~~~~~~~~~~~~~~~~~~~

I am writing this on the bus to Ouranopolis, where I'll get the motor launch for Daphne and Mount Athos. I am carrying what appears to be tons of gear. It seems inappropriate that I have so much equipment. A hermit fasting in a cave doesn't need much. Then why am I taking so much? It's not because I lack faith or resolve. It's because I'm scared and I am taking out insurance against emergencies.

Agios knows I'm going to Athos, but he doesn't know why. However he has the name and address of the administrator in Karyai who can get a message to me in case of emergency.

FRIDAY, 15 SEPTEMBER 1967
THESSALONIKI

~~~~~~~~~~~~~~~~~~~~~~~~

I am in Hotel Poulos in Thessaloniki — having gotten off the bus because I was frightened. It suddenly came to me that forty days is six weeks, and I thought, What, me not eat anything for six weeks? Me, alone in an almost inaccessible cave with nothing but water for six weeks? It terrified me because I realized that although I'm in comparatively good health now, I've been ailing for years. Can my fifty-seven-year-old hunk of flesh stand such a rigor? Suppose I become sick and am too weak to climb up the chain ladder out of the cave that hangs over a thousand-foot cliff?

I must have been crazy to have even considered "fasting for forty days in the wilderness" without first having had a physical examination. But what doctor is there who knows beans about fasting? Then I thought about Dr. Bishop Simonoptritus, Maria's uncle in Lesvos. The Greek Orthodox Church probably knows more about fasting than any organization in the world. So I got off the bus, came here, and cabled Maria: NEED PHYSICAL EXAMINATION BEFORE STARTING FORTY DAY FAST ATHOS. WILL YOUR BISHOP PHYSICIAN UNCLE DO IT? LOVE GEORGE ADAMSON POULOS HOTEL THESSALONIKI.

SATURDAY, 16 SEPTEMBER 1967

THESSALONIKI

~~~~~~~~~~~~~~~~~~~~~~~~~~~~~~

Maria telephoned this morning and told me that her uncle will be glad to not only examine me but also to instruct me on how to fast. Can I get to Lesvos on this afternoon's plane — there's one departs from Athens at four. Her uncle's scheduled to leave for Crete tomorrow.

I took the phone number and said if I didn't call her back in twenty minutes, I'd be on that plane. Good, she'd meet me.

I've just called the airline. There's space all the way. I'm already feeling a lot safer concerning my six-week water diet in the sacred dungeon. I shouldn't think so negatively. My "fasting for forty days in the wilderness" isn't a chore I'm being forced to do. It's something I *must* accomplish. It's an exploratory path on which I have an obsession to travel — as have a great many other people who were better and more worthy than I am.

SATURDAY, 16 SEPTEMBER 1967
MARIA'S VILLA
LESVOS

~~~~~~~~~~~~~~~~~~~~~~~~~~~~~~~~~~

The bishop was at Maria's when we arrived, sitting peacefully, smoking a pipe, and drinking wine. He jumped up, shook my hand vigorously, "Ah, you look much better. A new man," he said. "Absolutely a new man. Thank God." Then to Maria, "Hey, girl, when do we eat?"

"In about forty-five minutes. After we swim."

"Then let's have a look now, young man," he said, leading me into what had been my bedroom. The doctor-bishop listened to my heart, thumped me, felt me, took my pulse and blood pressure. While he was doing this, Maria came in, said that she was having a swim and that we could join her if we had time. She went out to the beach, saying, "See you soon."

Doctor-bishop packed his few instruments, said, "You'll soon be in as good condition as I am and I fast for five weeks every year before Christmas. Every fifteenth of November I go to the Holy Mountain. It's good for the body, mind, and soul to fast. It's equally good for God. We'll talk about it at dinner. Now let's swim." With that he took off his clothes and we, both naked, went to the beach.

The three of us swam to the point I knew so well — and back. It winded me, but my pride forced me to keep up. We walked from the sea to the house, all of us laughing and grunting happily, and we showered together outside the house.

At dinner the bishop, between mouthfuls, talked about fasting. "Fasting's important in the Orthodox Church — as important as prayer, as important as going to church, as important as the liturgy."

"Fasting isn't done to punish the flesh or for self-abasement. Lord, no! It's the opposite, I tell you. It's done for man's and God's joy — so that they can synergize. Body, mind, and spirit are a unity." He pointed outside toward the sea. "About five months ago, Giorgho, you couldn't swim from here to the point. Your body was almost dead and your soul smothered. You've still got a long way to go, yes, a long way, but there's a vitality now growing in you. At first I hardly recognized you. And after you're through fasting, your body and spirit will radiate with full health. God and your body and you will be a Trinity. How did your progress start? It began with Maria guiding you through exercise and fasting, It began with your body. Bless you, Maria, for what you've done. When Giorghos arrived here, he was a disgrace to God. Now he's on his way to becoming an icon. Ah, I wish I could travel to the Mountain with you, Giorgho. But to see God you must go alone. Bless you, Maria, for having helped him."

Maria reached across the table and touched her uncle's hand.

"Yes, Maria, I know. I'm beginning to spout with wind and thunder. All right, Giorgho, you're perfectly fit to fast for forty days."

The bishop then explained the routine of fasting. The body can go without food for six weeks as long as one drinks plenty of water. After six weeks it is dangerous. Not everyone needs to fast for forty days. The body will tell you when to resume eating. How does it tell you? The coating on the tongue clears away. The mucus in your nose dries up. You suddenly feel clean inside. You can feel your spirit working. You can talk with God. Then you can end your fast.

He discussed the discomforts to be expected. For the first few days the body will be restless and demand food. Get through the first few days, and the fast is heaven. At the beginning, during your discomfort, you may be angry, frustrated, bad-tempered. It is the evil, the poison starting to flow out. About this time you may experience a pounding of the heart — your pulse may increase to over a hundred. It's frightening, but is routine. It happens to almost everyone and only lasts for a few hours. About the seventh or eighth day you may feel weak and dizzy for an hour or two. The bishop said that because he's old — eighty-one — he takes a teaspoon or two of honey to raise his blood sugar level when he feels weak and dizzy, and in a little while, in two or three minutes, his infirmity has gone completely. He said that many poisons leave the body during the fast and, therefore, you must bathe often, several times a day, and you must drink much water. Perhaps ten or twelve glasses a day at least — throughout the entire fast. You must not do strenuous exercise during the fast — you will be weak. Still, you must do much exercise. He said, "I walk for an hour in the morning and again in late afternoon. Around noon, I sleep for several hours. When the fast is over, I break it slowly. Very slowly. I break my fast with one piece of fruit the first morning — or perhaps a handful of cooked grain. I increase this gradually, taking perhaps ten days before eating regularly." He lit his pipe, then added, "One more thing. Remember, this is a unique fast, a special fast, 'forty days in the wilderness.' The fasting you do in your home is of another nature. We can discuss that some other time."

That's the essense of what the bishop told me. I asked him what about the spiritual aspects of the fast. He smiled. "Your relations with God during the fast, well, who can tell how or whether the Spirit will visit you? Those questions you must answer yourself at the time. But always remember, your duty is to become God's image — His reflection — to be God's icon, so that God can see who He is. God needs you as much as you need God."

I was startled when he said that. I almost asked him if he'd read my book about God needing man, but I didn't. He stood up and came to me, put his hand on my shoulder and asked if I felt ill. No, I told him, I was just excited; and the feeling I had was inexpressible.

He said, "It's all absolutely inexpressible. It's one thing that neither God nor man can put into man's language. You and God must feel it together. No one can teach you." He looked at the big clock on the wall and said, "I must go. At five tomorrow my boat leaves for Crete."

After the bishop had left, I sat at the dining room table and began writing this journal; and at the same time thinking about what the bishop had said about God needing man as much as man needed God. I also thought about how astonished everyone seemed at the change in me. I'll have time to think about this while I'm fasting.

WEDNESDAY, 20 SEPTEMBER 1967

OURANOPOLIS

~~~~~~~~~~~~~~~~~~~~~~~~~~~~~~~~~~~~~

It has been three days since I left Lesvos. I am now in Ouranopolis, where the Athos Peninsula joins the mainland. A letter from Maria's uncle, the bishop, was waiting for me when I arrived at the hotel.

Dear Giorghos,

After you have gone through the official formalities at Karyai, from that moment on travel *on foot*. In these hectic and hurried days, almost everyone goes around the holy peninsula by motorboat, stopping at one monastery after another. Do not indulge yourself this way. You now are a seeker of the spirit and no longer a writer of books or a tourist sightseer. You must travel to your sacred spot the way the holy monks have done for over a thousand years, *on foot*, carrying your belongings on your back like God's donkey. In past millenia there were no motor launches to get from one monastery to another. The monks built paths of rock over the mountains, across the valleys, along the sides of the cliffs. Every stone step has been blessed, has been bathed in monks' hymns to God and in their perspiration and their love. This blessed energy still flows from those stone steps, and if you go on foot you will feel it, you will absorb it, you will be initiated by it.

It is a long, hard tiring walk from Karyai to your sacred cliff, about 40 kilometers. Do not hurry, even if you are able to. It's difficult to hurry over those rocky, twisting, up-and-down paths anyway, very difficult. My sacred fasting skete is not far from yours. Mine is just beyond St. Basil's, overlooking the island of Christophoros. I allow myself three days from Karyai to there.

I urge you to *walk*. If you try to hurry, your inner ears and inner eyes will miss much. Further, dear friend, even though you are fit to fast for forty days, your body is not fit to speed over the rough, steep, mountain paths without months of previous practice and training.

Pay heed that your holy experience begins the moment you depart Karyai. Your long walk the length of the holy peninsula is a preliminary that in some mysterious way will prepare you for your fasting experience.

I look forward to seeing you again, my dear brother,

Andrew Simonoptritus

Postscript: The Synodic Committee of Press and Opticoacoustics has seen your manuscript and is impressed. St. Anne's has been instructed to help you in all ways.

THURSDAY, 21 SEPTEMBER 1967
XEROPOTAMOU MONASTERY

~~~~~~~~~~~~~~~~~~~~~~~

At 6:45 A.M. I departed from Ouranopolis for Daphne and Karyai.

9:00 A.M.: Landed at Daphne harbor. Passport, etc. to police. About 11:00 A.M. to monastic capital, Karyai. Again to police station for registry — but policemen for foreigners would not be back until 2:30. Had lunch. Slept on sidewalk. Then unpacked my big old knapsack and made a final inventory of equipment. There are no stores outside of Karyai.

medical supplies for just about any emergency
tape recorder
Leica, film, light meter
5 stenographer's notebooks, pencils
Swiss army knife
30 feet mountain-climbing line for emergencies
toilet paper
sleeping bag

toilet articles
2 towels
flashlight, extra batteries
dungarees
heavy pants and shirt (Bishop advised it will be cold)
turtleneck sweater
watch cap
boots (I'll wear)
sneakers
two pairs woolen socks
one set heavy underwear (Bishop advised)
matches
canteen
poncho
wristwatch
woodsmens' bug lotion
pipe and tobacco
small jar of honey
emergency food — enough for five days
map of Athos
Bible
my red walking cane
extra glasses
ball of twine

I've repacked. The knapsack is heavy, 43 pounds. My weight is 159 pounds. I've lost 21 pounds since arriving in Greece. My weight in college was 152. The bishop said he loses about 8 kilograms (17 pounds) when he fasts. He's 81, very slender and normally eats little. If I lose 17 pounds, I'll come out of here weighing 142. Only twice in my life have I been under 150. Once I got to 149 when I was courting Sheila; and once I was 129 after having had mononucleosis.

At 4:45 I lifted my heavy load to my back and started for Xeropotamou Monastery — about 8 km distant.

Shortly after I left Karyai, two young hikers caught up with me, Andreas, (21) and Spiros, (20), who are walking around the entire peninsula and visiting all twenty monasteries. Both are considering becoming monks. Their first stop, like mine, was Xeropotamou, and they suggested we go together. They went at a very fast pace because the gates of the monastery are closed at sunset.

I am approximately three times as old as these young men and didn't want to be a drag on them, but then the thought of being locked out for the night spurred me too. I felt the muscles of my legs straining as I pushed myself to keep up. The heavy pack began chafing me just above the coccyx and perspiration dripped from my body.

Approaching Xeropotamou excited me. The graceful lines, the beautiful masonry, the perfectly balanced landscaping all indicated ancient genius. It was first built in 424. The great doors are thick and studded — for pirates and Arabs raided the monastery often. The vast building once housed over a thousand monks. Today there are twenty-nine, most of them old. The decline is heartbreaking. The viaducts and cisterns are muddy, sluggish, choked with debris.

Dinner at about 7:15. A bowl of soup with barley-sized pasta in it and anchovies and bread.

After dinner, the cook (a nonmonk) threw the garbage into the courtyard below.

FRIDAY, 22 SEPTEMBER 1967
ENROUTE TO GREGORIOU MONASTERY

~~~~~~~~~~~~~~~~~~~~~~~~~~~~~~~

Went to morning services at Xeroptamou at 4:30 A.M. They gave me a spiritual uplift; and even though there were only a dozen monks present, I felt the force of the thousands of others who had prayed and sung here for 1,500 years.

Andreas, Spiros, and I departed at 6:00 A.M. and went to Daphne harbor, which is about 4 km below the monastery. The boys took a shortcut down the old stone path — steep, filled with jutting boulders. On the way down, my legs and shoulders hurt, and I decided that after Daphne I'd do as the bishop had advised — walk slowly and alone. At Daphne I had bread and cheese for breakfast (Daphne and Karyai are the only places on the peninsula where there are restaurants or grocery stores).

It is now 8:00 A.M. My knee and hip joints scrape, and my muscles feel like dried-up rubber. Departed alone for Simonpetra, walking more slowly. Got there for lunch. Slept, and upon getting up at 4:30 P.M., decided to push on to Gregoriou Monastery. Was inclined to stay overnight because I hurt so much from the abrupt use of my still flabby muscles and from carrying this 43-pound pack of equipment. It now seems senseless bringing along all this junk. I'm a slave to camera, insect powders, food, film, etc. I have an impulse to go back to Karyai and leave everything except my clothes there.

FRIDAY, 22 SEPTEMBER 1967
GREGORIOU MONASTERY

T he walk from Simonpetra to Gregoriou wasn't long in length (about an hour and fifteen minutes for me), but it was down a very steep trail, and that utterly fatigued me. I could hardly put one foot in front of the other. At the bottom was a beautiful beach. Then up again. Up, up, up again, steep, steep, steep path. I thought, With this 43-pound pack, I'm like a donkey.

Just around the bend of the upward path I heard men talking, laughing. Then I saw them, about a dozen monks working. They carried heavy rocks, split them, dug up the hillside, and laid the rocks to make the path that hung on the side of the cliff.

One of them, roaring with laughter, shouted, "You're a donkey all right. You're one of God's donkeys. He's riding you and, I tell you, He's very heavy."

"We were God's donkeys too," said another monk. Some of them laughed, and a few of them looked serious. "But why are *you* loaded like a donkey?"

"This heavy pack," I said, "has a camera in it, canned food, rope, canteen, lots of things for my comfort and. . . ." I couldn't say it.

"And what?"

I found it hard to answer, but I did, "And for my ego."

The monks looked at each other questioningly. Had I translated the modern word *ego* properly into Greek? Of course I had. *Ego* = *I*. I continued. "Do I need these things to embrace the Holy Mountain? No I don't. Maybe I'm not God's donkey. Maybe it's Satan I'm carrying on my back? Maybe it's Satan who has fastened these knapsack girths around my donkey belly?"

"God and Satan look alike," said a monk. The others nodded in agreement.

I asked how one can tell them apart.

A monk pushed a stone into place, then said, "It's like going into a market. You look at the merchandise. If the merchant sells the merchandise to you at a cheap price, then he's Satan. But if you buy the cheap merchandise, it always burns your hands after you leave the market. If the merchant is God, the price is expensive, but the goods last forever."

Another monk said, "Ah, how tired you are. Let us help you."

"We can push you up the mountain," said another. "We can even make cold water gush from the rock — water to cool you. But the knapsack you must carry yourself. Or, if you decide to make the burden lighter, then you must throw the contents away yourself."

The monks began walking down the mountain and around the bend, probably looking for another place to repair. Soon I neither heard nor saw them. I continued up the twisting, steep path that led to Gregoriou Monastery.

On a particularly steep section, I stumbled — just from fatigue and daydreaming — and fell into a bush that lines the paths. It resembles holly and has prickles. My palms got pricked. Only little dots of blood, but, oh, how they itched!

I had been thinking, Yes, we're donkeys, going with our heavy loads up mountains and down and up again. But perhaps it's neither God nor Satan who rides our backs, digging spurs into our sides.

Perhaps it's us sitting on our own backs. Perhaps we're projections of both God and Satan. Whatever the heavy burden, it's there — that's no mistake. It hurts us and it slows us and it distracts us. Is it possible that we want it there? (Remember Cavafy's poem "Waiting for the Barbarians.")

SATURDAY, 23 SEPTEMBER 1967
GREGORIOU MONASTERY

~~~~~~

The cleanliness here at Gregoriou reminds me of "cleanliness is next to godliness." There is a scrubbed look about the place; indeed, the entire monastery has a hard-working, deep-praying atmosphere. I went to bed at 8:30 P.M. and was up at 2:30 A.M. with the ringing of the monastery bells. Church services began at 3:00 A.M. By 4:50 I found myself falling asleep, so I left and went back to bed, still very tired, stiff, and aching.

SATURDAY, 23 SEPTEMBER 1967
ENROUTE TO ST. ANNE'S MONASTERY

~~~~~~~~~~~~~~~~~~~~~~~~~~~~~

I decided to push on to St. Anne's. My inclination was to stop
overnight at one monastery after another in order to rest.
But this was not, I concluded, what the bishop meant by
"going slowly." *Walk slowly* was what he had said. When I stay
overnight at monasteries I am dawdling. Because of my research in
the monasteries, I know many monks; and they are glad to see me
back; and they like to talk. Most of them know I've finished the book,
and so they're curious as to why I've returned and am traveling with
a knapsack instead of returning to *Varvaros* at night. I don't want to
discuss my forty days of fasting in the wilderness. I have a feeling that
my adventure will be wrecked if I talk about it. At Karyai, the
administrator assured me that only two monks (both at St. Anne's)
had been informed of what I was doing: the abbot and the old monk
who had taken me to the cave when I, as a writer, had requested to
see some of the "wilderness sketes."

I smile as I recall how firmly the bishop had warned me to *walk
slowly*. In my present condition, I have no choice. I learned that

214

simple lesson a few days ago during the hour or so burst of speed I had when I galloped along with Andreas and Spiros from Karyai to Xeropotamou — about five miles. The fact is that I hurt all over even when I walk slowly, especially when climbing the mountain steps; and when one moves on Athos, there's nothing else but mountain steps. It is better for me if I walk slowly and steadily until I reach my destination, and not make overnight stops along the way.

And so I've decided to go from Gregoriou directly to St. Anne's. What with resting along the way, eating, and perhaps sleeping a little, I figure I'll make the 15-km trip in about seven hours. I'll stay at St. Anne's overnight (after seeing the abbot and the old monk, who has been directed to come and check on me every two weeks) and then tomorrow proceed to St. Anthimus' cave — *my* cave. My excitement and my awe increase as I wonder why the old monk hadn't permitted me to look inside the cave, telling me that only those on religious missions were permitted to enter. I asked the administrator at Karyai about this. He gave an expression that is characteristically Greek — a half-smile, half-frown — and answered that there are some relics that should be reserved for the soul, not for the idle curiosity of the thousands of tourists who come to Athos on their vacations every year. I told him that no tourist could possibly find that wild hidden skete. He gave me another half-smile, half frown, said, "Even so," and went about checking my papers.

SATURDAY, 23 SEPTEMBER 1967

ST. ANNE'S MONASTERY

~~~~~~~~~~~~~~~

I hoisted the knapsack on George-the-donkey and started for St. Anne's. Went the approximately 5 km to Dionysiou, rested for half-hour, then went on about 4 km to the vicinity of St. Paul's, rested and ate bread, cheese, a tomato that I'd gotten at Gregoriou. Then got lost on the way to New Skete, but went back in the direction of the sea and found a path that led to New Skete. To make certain I didn't get lost going up the mountain to St. Anne's, I knocked on a house door to get directions. A fat, dirty monk answered. He seemed irritated, perhaps supposing I was going to ask if I could stay there overnight. He appeared relieved when I asked for St. Anne's; and seeing how exhausted I looked, he gave me some ouzo, jam, and coffee. He then walked me to a path that went (it seemed to me) almost vertically up the mountain, pointed, and said, "Saint Anne's."

The pack went on the donkey's back again, and up the mountain I started. It was so steep and I was so tired that I stopped every five minutes to catch my breath, and every fifteen minutes to take the pack off the donkey's back, stretch out, and rest.

But with each step, I felt more and more joyful in spirit. I thought, What have I done to deserve such joy? I've hurt so many people, have been so selfish, have told so many lies. Even today I've told lies (temporarily believing them myself). Despite all this, I'm being blessed more and more with the passing of each minute — and I do not understand it.

But I found myself accepting the unearned blessings as a gift; and I felt thankful.

I reached St. Anne's at sunset. The view here is a geographic nirvana. In front, way below, is the sea. In the rear is the fierce-looking mountain.

My heels are blistered. I've removed my boots and put on the more comfortable sneakers. The air is chilly, and I am cold.

Halfway up here I thought about Papa. Even though I don't remember him very well, I recalled his once saying that his dream was to be alone for about a month, hiking in the mountains and roughing it — not seeing anyone, so that he could think in peace. I thought, Well, here was one thing that my father wanted to do and never did — and I, his son, am doing it. I wondered if my carrying out one of his dreams would please him.

At that moment I had a dull pain in my chest. Could it have been because I associate heart problems with my father and his death? Or perhaps doctor-bishop's diagnosis wasn't accurate and I really have a heart problem? Or have I got some guilt feelings over doing something that Papa was unable to accomplish? No, it couldn't be that. When a younger generation does what the older failed in, it should be a time for rejoicing. It was at that time I came to a fork in the path and had to decide which path to continue on; and I forgot about my heart (the pain in my chest disappeared), and I stopped thinking about my father. I took the left fork because it seemed most traveled. A few minutes later I saw the St. Anne's compound. The monastery is an architectural jewel.

SUNDAY, 24 SEPTEMBER 1967
ST. ANNE'S MONASTERY
~~~~~~~~~~~~~~~~~~~~~~~~~~~

T his morning about 4:45 the old monk came to my room,
roused me, and said that we were to meet with the abbot
at 5:00.

We met in the dining hall and talked while we ate breakfast —
a small cup of Turkish coffee, a shot of raki, a square of sweet candy,
and some bread.

"Veniamin here," said the abbot, glancing at the old monk, "will
lead you to your cave."

I protested, saying I'd prefer to go alone.

"Yes, yes, I understand. But," he said, holding a letter up, "we have
an interest in you and the cave is well-hidden, hard to find. There
is no path. There is danger if you get lost." He smiled at me. "You
will make me more comfortable if you accept Veniamin's guidance."

Veniamin stroked his long white beard and said nothing.

I nodded.

"Once you are there, he will leave you, of course. In two weeks
he will return just to see how you are. Suppose you are ill or break

a leg or, in your walks, meet demons? It will make us all more comfortable to know you are well and prospering in God's love."

I nodded again. Both monks smiled and stood up. Veniamin stroked his white beard again — it came to his chest — and said, "When would you like to start?"

"When are the services?"

"In a few minutes. They'll be over in an hour."

"May we start then?"

The abbot filled our small raki glasses, held his glass up in a toast and said, "For the love of God."

SUNDAY, 24 SEPTEMBER 1967

ENROUTE TO ST. ANTHIMUS' CAVE

~~~~~~~~~~~~~~~~~~~~~~~~~~~~~~~

F
or me it was a hard climb, and I rested perhaps every fifteen minutes. The old monk was very patient. Just before the path forked to the left up to Kerasia and the peak, Veniamin pointed to a newly driven stake on the right. There was no path, but he turned there and said this was the way. Through the bushes we went, up a steep incline to the right. About every two hundred yards there was a newly driven stake.

"To make certain you can find your way," he said.

We went on, up over smaller peaks for about half an hour (although in my excitement, I really didn't notice how much time passed). Then down a steep slope an equal distance to the edge of the cliff that dropped to the sea.

"We are here?" I asked.

"Yes, there it is."

He took off his light rucksack, handed it to me and said it contained a few things I might need; and that I could return them when I left. He pointed to some bushes and told me that when I felt weak I could boil their leaves and would be refreshed. I said I had not brought a pot.

"There is one in the bag," he said. "And the spring is over here. Come, I'll show you." He led me to the spring, about twenty feet away. He hugged me, kissed me, said, "God will be with you." Then he started back up the mountain. When he was almost out of sight, he waved, then turned and disappeared into the forest.

That was fifteen minutes ago. I am sitting here alone, writing and trying to get the courage to enter the cave. Also I am very hungry. In my pack are olives, bread, cheese from St. Anne's. Should I have my last meal before I climb down to the cave?

I ate everything. I took the small pot from the rucksack, got some water from the spring. I poured some powdered coffee into it, stirred it, and drank it cold, smoking my pipe.

Then I got on my knees and gave thanks. I thanked everyone who directly or indirectly had made my adventure, my exploration, possible — the bishop-doctor, Maria, Ziggy, Agios, Sheila, Gregory, Alexis, Ito, and Constantine and *Varvaros,* and others. I thanked myself. Then I looked about and with all my senses embraced the trees, the sea, the rocks, the sun, the grass, the mysterious vitality of the cosmos (yes! I experienced that sensually) and I thanked them. It was in this manner that I thanked that supreme vitality that we call God.

I ARRIVE AT CAVE
SUNDAY, 24 SEPTEMBER 1967

〰〰〰〰〰〰〰〰〰

The cave is in the face of the cliff; the roof is about four feet from the top. The floor of the cave is perhaps ten feet from the top of the cliff. In front of the cave is a ledge, a natural verandah that juts out eight or nine feet over the ocean hundreds of feet below. An old ladder made of chain is bolted into the cliff on top and leads down to the ledge.

I looked down and panicked. I have fear of heights. I become faint and, at the same time, feel the thrust of the well known inclination to throw one's self out into space.

How could I possibly get up the courage to climb down the side of the cliff to the ledge and the cave? I tested the bolts that held the rusty, iron chain ladder. The bolts were about ten inches long, simply thrust into holes drilled into the rock. They could easily be pulled out, but they'd hold the chain ladder as long as the pull was downward and steady. How old was the rusty chain? I found no place that seemed to be corroded all the way through. Then I thought: If the abbot had taken the trouble to stake the path, he certainly must have tested the chain ladder.

I knew I had to go down it; and I felt that I could do it so long as I didn't look down at the rocky beach and ocean many hundreds of feet below.

About four feet from the edge of the cliff, above the cave, is a small tree. I ran my mountain-climbing line around the tree, then looped it about my knapsack and the monk's small rucksack and, holding on to the ends, lowered the packs to the ledge. That worked fine.

Then I tied the line under my arms — so that if the chain ladder parted, the line would hold me. I got on my belly, my feet dangling over the cliff, grabbed the top of the chain ladder, and moved myself toward the abyss inch by inch (all the while trembling with fright and wondering if it wouldn't be wise to chuck this whole deal and find myself a safer place in which to fast). I put one foot on the chain rung and tested it. It held me. I put both feet on the rungs, desperately holding on with my hands. I saw my knuckles, white and purple from pressure. I went down another step. Now my body was vertical, with all the weight on the chain. Another step, and another.

I reached the ledge, perspiration dripping from me despite the cool breeze. I was afraid to look down. I was afraid to stand up. I crawled into the cave as far as the line would allow — about ten feet. I sat there in the semidarkness for several minutes, breathing hard, but gradually feeling safer.

I pulled the packs in, got out my flashlight. Then I took the rope sling off — making certain the ends were tied together — so that I'd be certain to have a way of getting back up to the top of the cliff.

I stood up — there was about two feet of head room — and with the flashlight on walked toward the back of the cave. It seemed about thirty feet deep. There were some objects at the back.

On the rear wall was an altar with a gold cross. Also on the altar were three skulls. This didn't startle me because I knew that the skulls of hermits often were placed in the caves where the hermits had lived for many years. It didn't startle me, but it stirred me. I felt as if I were going to spend the next six weeks in a mausoleum and that I'd not be alone. Also on the altar was a portable icon of Mary and Jesus. It was very beautiful, and from the shadings of the rich blues and the composition it well could have been a Panselinos; and I recalled how the monasteries had hidden their treasures in caves when the Nazis invaded Greece.

I walked to the front of the cave, got on my hands and knees and carefully crept out to the windy ledge. I forced myself to look down; and I felt as if some force were shoving me, urging me to fling myself out into space. I heard myself say aloud, "Get thee from behind me, Satan," and with that I began laughing. Still laughing, I stood up, walked back into the cave. Near the wall was a small, crude fireplace of stones and next to it was a small heap of twigs, very dry and old. I wondered how old they were.

The reason I was laughing was that when I had had the inclination to fling myself off the ledge and into space, I had said, "Get thee from behind me, Satan," and then a moment later had added, "Yes, Satan, you stay in front of me where I can keep an eye on you."

Even though I was laughing there was something profound here. Perhaps it was that we should remain aware of our strange temptations, not just shovel them underneath our consciousnesses and pretend they don't exist.

I sat down by the fireplace, wondering how many hermits ahead of me (yes, I am a hermit now) had cooked over that small fireplace, had warmed themselves in front of it. I also wondered what Veniamin had brought me in his rucksack. I opened it. There were two dozen fat candles, a small hatchet, three cans of corned beef, about a dozen slices of hard crunchy bread, a bottle of raki, a small crucifix for hanging around my neck, matches, a pair of gloves.

His generosity moved me. I walked out to the entrance (carefully putting the line cradle around me), stepped on to the ledge and forced myself to look down and around. I said aloud, "Push all you want, Satan, you can't get me off this ledge into space. You know why? Because my friend Veniamin is looking after me."

Then I went in, lit a fire, made coffee, wolfed a can of corned beef, two slices of Veniamin's crunchy bread, and had a big slug of raki. "My fasting," I said, "can start tomorrow. Today I'm still a pig."

I belched a few times, then went to the rear, stroked the skulls of my cavemates, got on my knees in front of the altar, and admired the beautiful gold cross and the beautiful icon. On the bottom of the icon was written: ALL-POWERFUL LORD, WE FEAR THY WRATH. HAVE MERCY ON US, WRETCHED SINNERS ALL.

I returned to where my knapsack was, untied my sleeping bag, laid it out, crawled into it, said, "Screw you, Satan," and prepared myself for sleep.

MONDAY, 25 SEPTEMBER 1967
ST. ANTHIMUS' CAVE

~~~~~~~~~~~~~~~~~~~~~~~~~~~~~~

S lept all yesterday and most of the night. Awakened in the dark, not knowing where I was. No hints except the cold, hard, rock floor. Gradually I remembered. The darkness is absolute — no stars, no distant streetlamp to provide even a glimmer of light. I switched on the flashlight — 4:13 A.M. My watch is my only link to civilization. Well, there's the flashlight; but even with extra batteries it may not last more than a few weeks.

It's colder than I had expected. I must get some wood and keep a small fire going.

About 5 A.M. I had to go to the toilet. Where? There was only one place — on the ledge in front of the cave. I'd clean up the mess in full daylight.

THE WATER PROBLEM

~~~~~~~~~~~~~~~~~

I foraged about an eighth of a cord of twigs today. I've been
damned hungry; and by early afternoon had a headache;
and my mouth tasted like a garbage pail. Every time I think
of food, I drink water — which is about every fifteen minutes. Four
canteens full — about sixteen glasses. The tiny spring only holds
about two quarts and refills at a trickle. The last two canteens of water
were muddy. I tried to bathe but the best I could do was wet the end
of a towel and rub myself. I must find another source of water.

I followed the stakes out to the Lavra path. Near where the path
forks to the left toward the peak is a pipe pouring out a steady stream
of water.

TUESDAY, 26 SEPTEMBER 1967
ST. ANTHIMUS' CAVE

~~~~~~

For over forty hours I haven't eaten. No ill effects. I am realizing what an enormous amount of time, effort, and money we spend on meals. Now that I am fasting, the social functions of eating become apparent. The way one eats, the place, the food, the cooking equipment, the people we eat with — all these often are status symbols. This symbol stuff is bought, sold, and advertised as a commodity in today's culture. Eating often is a form of entertainment, often an activity to avoid boredom. Sometimes it is a way of getting a bit of self-security; especially for those who have low satisfaction levels in other activities or relationships.

For primitive man, the very act of obtaining food — which frequently involved danger — was a triumph. It was synonymous with survival; therefore eating, for early man, became an exultant, jubilant pleasure. However today, for many, eating is an emotional crutch — a method of enlarging and feeding the ego. Is this why the saints fasted for forty days (the maximum safe time) — that is, *as a means of diminishing the ego?* And did they do it alone in the wilderness so that they'd receive no social applause for their fortitude and sacrifice? But then how is it that we know of their fasting? They must have told someone. Perhaps fasting in the wilderness for forty days is in itself a supreme form of ego glutting? When society hears about it, the faster is diagnosed either as a hero or an idiot. This includes, of course, Moses, Jesus, Buddha and, incidentally, me.

Is this what being spiritual is all about — the elimination of the ego? If so, perhaps this is why Jesus arranged his own crucifixion? He was becoming popular and well-known through his miracles of healing. He even had twelve disciples — twelve press agents — who considered him the messiah (one who would defeat the enemies, give the disciples power, and supply them with all the pleasures of "heaven"). Perhaps poor Jesus, when he realized this, manipulated his crucifixion as the ultimate act of ego elimination? If this is true, it is sufficient reason to worship him as a hero and a symbol, indeed, a creator of élan vital.

I'm now having doubts about *my* fasting in the wilderness. I believed I was motivated by the desire to learn what started some of the holy people on the path to sainthood. Perhaps my project is, instead, a well camouflaged ego orgy? Perhaps even sainthood is a camouflaged ego orgy? Jesus advised us that our fasting, our praying, and our charitable acts should be done in secret. If we publicize them (or allow them to be publicized), then we receive applause and admiration — thus glutting the ego. When this happens, *Diavolas* cunningly has outsmarted us in the name of sainthood.

Is Loneliness Powerful?

I am lonely for communications with other living things. In the cave are all kinds of spiders, and so I go around in the late afternoon when the sun shines in and I say hello to the spiders. They move up and down their webs when I speak. I guess this is spider language; however, as yet, I haven't learned it.

Is my loneliness making my inner eye keener? When I walk I think I can see the luminosity — the auras — around the trees, bushes, and the earth itself. I feel that they are talking to me. I hold out my arms and say, "All of you, I love you." And when I do that I see streamers of energy (they look like heat waves) stretching to me and embracing me. When I am tired and weak, this strengthens and nourishes me; and I do it daily. Is this real? If so, is this the prana, the life force, that, according to legend, feeds the hermits in the Himalaya during the years when they eat no ordinary food?

I have begun talking to trees, rocks, brooks; and with my inner ears I hear them reply; and sometimes what they say is startling. I told the big beech near the Lavra path spring that because it couldn't move, I'd describe to it interesting places and things I've seen on my travels — the banyan trees in Asia, the rain forests of the Amazon, the evergreens near my farm in New Hampshire. The beech tree answered, "There's more to see here than one can digest in a lifetime. It's only the blind who are compulsive travelers."

So — because of my loneliness — I'm enlarging my repertoire of acquaintances. I'm sensing that everything pulses with life force, even inanimate objects; and that they have languages — silent though they might be. Still, one can hear them. Is this what the bishop meant when he mentioned "the inner ears"?

Although these things are a joy to me, my only truly intimate friend is my wristwatch — an old friend of fifteen years, a Patek Philippe that cost me $1,000 in Hong Kong in 1952. We've been all over the world together, the watch, the knapsack, and myself. The watch is alive and it speaks a language I can hear and see. I wind it; and its hands move for me at a predictable and interpretable rate. Between the watch and me there is synergy. I time my pulse, my walks, my work periods, my sleep time with the help of my friend the watch.

I was chilly last night and caught a small cold. Nevertheless, this noon I went for a walk and ended up climbing to the peak and back, which took me six hours. I overdid it. Now as I lie here, there is a dull pain in the general area of my heart, which is pounding hard; and my pulse is 108. I am breathing deeply because someone told me that makes the heart's work easier. Yogi breathing. Slow, deep, using the diaphragm.

I am wondering what to do if it gets worse? Get up and climb and stumble the twelve miles to Lavra where there's a doctor — or the six miles to St. Anne's, where there is no doctor? Or stay here in my sleeping bag and hope that rest will help.

Maybe the pain in my heart area is from gas? Whatever, it seems to be getting worse, and it frightens me.

If I should die tonight, when will my death be discovered? When Veniamin comes to check on me in a few days? Would decomposition have begun to set in? I have the inclination to get up and put my clothes and gear in order, all of which now is scattered in a slovenly manner about the cave.

The sensation in my chest is dull, not sharp. It is not excruciatingly painful, but it is deep. The general area is about seven inches below the clavicle, left of the breastbone.

Now is the time when it would be a comfort to not be alone — to have someone here who loves me and whom I love. I suppose we all have the inclination to share our imperfections with people we love; and death is the ultimate imperfection. I don't expect to die tonight, but I am afraid; and at this moment I am terribly lonely. But if I were certain that the sensation in my chest is a coronary and that death might come this evening, then whom would I want to have here with me? Whose presence would make my frightened lips stop quivering — and perhaps help them to turn upward in a hopeful smile? Whose presence would be a comfort to me?

I feel as if I am skirting death. My mind involuntarily reviews my entire past. My total ocean of life experiences is distilled into a cupful of essence. To me, who may be dying, this essence appears precious; and I want to bequeath it to someone I love and trust. I see my entire life in a translucent cup. To whom do I want to give this cup? But who is there who loves me enough to *want* to sit with me when I am dying?

Who? Ah, here is a giant of a question.

You — who want to sit here with me while I am dying — you, — who also are the one I've chosen — come tell me about a time we laughed together; a time we shared a sorrow or a defeat or a triumph; a time we vigorously worked together and with cunning outsmarted our antagonist. Tell me about a time when we were foolish or stupid or about a time when we were wise and profound.

Whom do I wish to have here while I die? Who can both laugh and weep with me? I am not ashamed to crave this when I am dying.

I will not write out the very short guest list. This amuses me — a guest list for a death party. I will not put the name or names in this journal. Suppose I'm dead by morning? Others may read my list; and I don't want that. The list is only for the invited and me.

Ah, but the question! The answer to it tells me secrets about myself, secrets I've never thought about before — a list of those in whose presence I am happy to die. And how will I feel about them if I am alive tomorrow?

And if I am alive tomorrow, I must not forget that death will come some day; and so, in reality, I'll be dying slowly every day. The death scene may last for many years. Now, think about the question again: with whom do I want to be when I'm dying? And who would like to be with me then?

Tears are trickling down my cheek. Oh, God, I can't think of anyone. Not a single one.

T he sensation around my heart is still present, but diminished. If it isn't gone within several days, I'll walk very slowly to Lavra.

The reminder I've had of the imminence of death has helped clear my perspective. It now is easier to classify things in order of importance. Is so-and-so important? If not, forget about it.

But, whoa! Shouldn't I define what I mean by "importance"? This is difficult because importance is relative and constantly changing; and it varies with individuals. For example the most important thing for Tom is to get enough money to return to college. For Martha, it is to have a healthy baby born to her next month. For Agios, it is to publish good books that are best sellers. But for me, *at this moment,* it is most important to keep breathing, to go to the toilet, and to clean up the mess in this cave. In that order.

The pain is gone. However, I stayed in the cave all day and rested.

~~~~~~

L ast night I was cold again — the autumn wind from the sea bites — and I'm thinking that staying in this absurd cave is crazy. Sleeping on the chilly, stone floor is damned uncomfortable. If I have a bowel movement at night, I go out on the ledge that hangs over that terrible straight drop into the ocean. I'm always terrified lest I go out too far and fall off; and the next morning I push the main mess over the edge and scrub up the remainder with water and branches. It's remarkable that one has bowel movements even when one doesn't eat for almost two weeks — what a cesspool our guts are!

To stay warm I have to haul wood down — which means going up and down the blasted rickety chain ladder — and I am scared with every step. I have to make trips up and down, up and down, for firewood and water. The spring is the size of a small wash basin and takes half an hour to fill up. And every time I leave here for a walk I pack the safety line, the hatchet, flashlight, the canteen, and matches. It's easy to get lost, and there are many hidden ravines.

Certainly I'm not here fasting to punish or immolate myself. This experience is supposed to be an illuminating joy both for God and me. Then why did I choose this most difficult and uncomfortable of places? Probably because I wanted to be a hero. The old ego again. All I want is to fast in joy and without distraction; but the physical hardships in this cave are major distractions. However, at this stage I have no options — at least not for several days until Veniamin comes. Certainly he'll know of a more comfortable hideout. I hope so.

Yes, after the first few days the food fasting is easy. It's the ego fasting that's difficult. The ego-fat has accumulated over half a century; and the mind is more difficult to discipline than the stomach.

For several days I've had a rash on my wrists, arms, and chest. Very itchy and tender, but it doesn't worry me. The bishop-doctor predicted it — it's the toxins leaving the body as fasting cleans me out. The only thing that bothers me is I can't wear my wristwatch. It chafes the wrist. I carry the watch in my shirt pocket.

I'm drinking about four quarts of water daily to hasten the cleansing process. Also, now that I've found a good water supply, I'm bathing more thoroughly, even though taking the bath requires about an hour of walking. But I make myself walk about four hours daily anyway. At noon, I sleep for two or three hours. My energy level is noticeably lower since I started fasting.

FRIDAY, OCTOBER 6 1967
ST. ANTHIMUS' CAVE

I've been taking my walks by following the line of stakes that leads to the Lavra path. Today I decided to go to the water supply by another route, to explore a bit. I headed northeast instead of north. There was no path, so I notched a tree every few minutes just in case I got lost.

About an hour from the cave, the ground abruptly dropped and I saw a deep, round pocket shaped like an amphitheater. It was about six hundred feet deep and about five hundred feet across, with steep, heavily wooded sides. But the bottom was smooth rock and resembled a slightly tilted concave mirror; this mirror pointed toward one of the sides. I decided to explore this strange amphitheater and started looking for the easiest way to descend into it, when suddenly I heard frightful moaning and high-pitched screaming coming from one end of the big pit. After about a minute, it stopped as abruptly as it had started.

I climbed down about fifty feet, and the deep moans and high-pitched screams started again. I wondered if a donkey had fallen down and injured itself. No, it couldn't possibly be an animal or a human being — the volume was too great. Then I wondered about the demons that the abbot at St. Anne's had mentioned.

As I got closer to the bottom, I saw a cave opening in the area from which the moans and screams were coming. For a moment, it occurred to me that someone was being murdered — but the pitch and volume were beyond the capacity of any human throat. I continued down. True, I was scared; but I don't believe in spooky stuff. Everything is a physiological phenomenon. Unknown things only become spooky when we don't understand them and when we become afraid. I wasn't frightened of the supernatural, but I was wary and nervous because I was alone.

It took me about twenty minutes to get to the rocky bottom — on the side away from the moaning and screaming — which which bellowed out intermittently. A few minutes of the horrible noises and then a few minutes of silence. But as I reached the bottom and started walking in the direction of the cave, the moaning and screaming stopped. I walked the several hundred feet slowly; and on the way got out my flashlight and safety line. As I neared the entrance, I walked very slowly, watching every step, alert — like David approaching Goliath. About ten feet from the entrance I stopped. In front of the entrance was a three-foot stone cube with well-defined chisel marks on its sides. It looked like a place to sit. On the left of the cave was a small masonry aqueduct — about a foot in diameter; and a small stream of water flowed from it into a small pool with masonry sides. The cave's opening was about ten by ten feet. Everything was quiet now except the whispering of the small stream of water flowing into the pool.

I secured the safety line around my waist and tied the other end of it around the square rock. I went to the entrance, switched on my flashlight. About twenty feet inside there was what seemed to be a low masonry platform about eight by three feet in length and width. My flashlight wasn't strong enough to illuminate beyond that point, but I estimated the cave went back at least forty or fifty feet.

I started in. As I entered I tripped and fell forward to the ground — and at that moment the moans and screams blasted from the far side of the cave. The moan was deep like a steamer's siren. The scream was like a high note on a calliope. At the same time, a cough of dank air swished out, and the breath was pungent, the smell of rotting vegetation and iodine.

I jumped up and ran out; and as I did, I saw what I had tripped over was a small masonry wall about six inches high — but hidden on the outer side by leaves and grass. It was manmade, its stones neatly held together with mortar.

The moaning and screaming and bad breath of the monster — or whatever it was — continued until I was outside, and then it stopped. Then, as I stood there, it began again. I noticed that it came from a fixed point within the cave, way at the back; and it sounded like an organ — or some sort of a giant wind instrument. It was not from a living thing. There was no tremolo, no variation in pitch or volume. Then it stopped again.

The silence continued for perhaps ten minutes. I stood outside the entrance, collecting myself and thinking.

I reentered, moving ahead slowly, looking down and then around with each step forward. I got to the back of the cave, twenty-seven paces, and there on the floor were two holes, one about two feet in diameter and the other about four inches, both irregular in shape. I put the light in them and saw that they went way down, far beyond the flashlight's beam. Then a breeze blew up through them — with the same pungent odor — and then the goddam noise came. From the big hole came a basso profundo foghorn bellow, and from the other came a high-pitched scream. It lasted for only about ten seconds and then the breeze and the roaring ceased.

Now it became clear. The holes must be the top of long subterranean passages leading through the mountain of rock all the way to the cliffs — probably coming out near the water level; and the long, twisted passages probably were acting like organ pipes.

I put my head down into the big hole and listened. I heard a faint, far away sound like waves breaking on rocks perhaps a mile away.

Then, my head still in the hole, the breeze came, and the shock of noise nearly knocked me out. It was unendurable and sounded like a thousand-decibel level.

The breeze and the noise stopped. I flashed the light on the holes. I saw two stones close to them. They were approximately the size of the holes. I pushed the big one over and saw that someone, with a chisel, had cut it to precisely the right size for fitting in the irregularly shaped hole. I jiggled it into place. Another breeze came, but only from the small hole, which gave forth its terrible high-pitched scream. I put the small stone in it; this stone also had been cut and shaped to fit the hole snugly. The screaming stopped. I lifted the small stone. The screaming started, but stopped when I again put the stone in place.

Having silenced the demons, I took a candle from my pack, lit it, and methodically began inspecting the cave.

Someone of intelligence, a skilled stonemason, had lived here. The raised platform was simply a rectangular eighteen-inch wall; and inside it was filled with twigs and leaves, all old and crumbled. I pushed around in it — it was soft. Probably a bed. I lay down in it and it was very comfortable. The small masonry wall at the entrance, about six inches high, obviously had been built to keep water out. About five feet from the bed was an ingenious stove-fireplace constructed from small, flat rocks. On one side was an oven. At the bottom was an opening designed to create a draft. A square stone was next to the hole — by moving it sideways, the draft could be controled. There were no smoke smudges on the overhead — in contrast to my cave which has soot all over.

A craftsman, a civilized person had lived here. He had discovered that it was a warm place in winter because the tilted, smooth, concave bottom of the amphitheater probably reflected the sun's heat to this spot. He had built a water supply. And on the hill behind the cave was a forest that provided wood.

Against the right wall of the cave, near the back, a long bin with three compartments had been constructed from stone and mortar. Perhaps for storing produce? Over it, in exquisitely beautiful lettering, was carved in the granite: GENTLE LORD, I THANK THEE FOR THY ENDLESS BOUNTY.

I went outside and looked around. On one side of the cave was a small aqueduct and pool, also stone-lined. On the other side there was a low stone wall surrounding a space that looked as if it had been a garden — although bushes and saplings now crowded it.

I was exhausted now — probably as much from the excitement as from physical exertion. I went back in and removed the stones from the "noise holes" and left. I started climbing the hill, having just about made up my mind to move to this comfortable cave; and as I had this thought, the moaning and screaming started again; and I estimated it easily could be heard at least a half-mile away.

By the time I got to the top of the hill I was stumbling like a drunkard from exhaustion. Would I have any problem getting "home" before dark? I looked at my wrist and then remembered that my watch was in my shirt pocket — it was 4:31. I'd better get back as quickly as possible. But because my canteen was empty, I decided to fill it from the spring on the Lavra path. It would only take a few minutes longer.

When I got to the spring, I was numb with fatigue; after all, I hadn't eaten for twelve days. I filled the canteen and then leaned over and held my head beneath the pipe from which the icy-cold water gushed. The shock of it revived me. I did it again — and then walked along the Lavra path until I saw the stakes, which marked the shortest way back.

The moment I got down the chain ladder, I started for the sleeping bag, and on the way I looked at the beautiful icon on the altar; and for the first time, the lettering on the bottom meant something to me: ALL-POWERFUL LORD, WE FEAR THY WRATH. HAVE MERCY ON US, WRETCHED SINNERS ALL.

And I recalled the exquisite lettering cut into the granite in the other cave: GENTLE LORD, I THANK THEE FOR THY ENDLESS BOUNTY. Then and there, I made up my mind to move to the other cave in the morning.

SATURDAY, 7 OCTOBER 1967

ST. ANTHIMUS' CAVE

MY LAST NIGHT WITH ST. ANTHIMUS

~~~~~~

This morning I took my gear from St. Anthimus' woeful, uncomfortable cave and lugged it to the top of the cliff. I stowed the equipment in my pack and then loaded the forty-three pounds onto George-the-donkey. When I started walking, I knew how weak the fasting had made me, even though I felt healthy; and I had the impression that my body and mind both were cleaner and sweeter than they had been a couple of weeks ago.

The pack felt so heavy and clumsy that I had difficulty walking. I thought about unloading half of it and making two trips. But my excitement was so high that I stumbled along with the full load, making happy noises. At first I simply brayed — experimenting until I had the donkey call almost authentic, then I brayed, honked and tootled louder than ever and shouted, "Make way for God's donkey! Make way for God's joyful two-legged donkey!" Then I made up happy songs about the glory of God, the goodness of life, and the great love-energy of the cosmos. Every tree, every stone, every plant poured out vitality and helped me along the rocky, precipitous way. Was I intoxicated with fasting?

What seemed to be hours later, I heard the moaning and screaming way off in my concave valley. In about fifteen minutes, I was at the crest of the hill and the moans and screams that once had sounded so scary and horrible now were like my own private symphony.

When I reached the mouth of *my* cave, I recalled that by tomorrow morning my first two weeks of "fasting in the wilderness" would be over, and Veniamin would be arriving at St. Anthimus' cave to check up on me. If neither I nor my gear were there, the abbot of St. Anne's would have searching parties scurrying all over the peninsula. I had to go back and be there. And because Veniamin would be there very early, it would be wise, I decided, for me to return to the cliff immediately and stay at St. Anthimus' overnight.

I stuffed my sleeping bag, safety line, flashlight, and canteen into the knapsack — leaving everything else in my new cave — and began hiking back to the cliff. I got there just before sunset and looked for my watch to see what time it was. But I couldn't find the watch. I looked in every pocket, turning them inside out — there was no watch.

Well, after Veniamin departs tomorrow, I'll search every inch of the route between here and the new cave. I'd had the watch this morning, so it has to be somewhere between here and there.

I couldn't sleep last night. The cold wind roared throughout the cave as if St. Anthimus were scolding me for deserting him; and I shivered even though I was in my sleeping bag and wore all my clothes. The energy in that cave is harsh and negative. Staying there for any length of time is almost an act of self-flagellation or immolation. Why do hermits, anchorites, punish themselves by hiding in cruel environments and physical discomforts? Do they think they're bribing God? Or do they simply hate themselves? Or do they feel incapable of living among other people? Or are they they just trying to give themselves an ego-enema?

I wonder if I should ask those questions of myself?

SUNDAY, 8 OCTOBER 1967

SKOPIAS' CAVE

~~~~~~~~~~~~~~~~~~~~~~

A little after sunrise I climbed the chain ladder for the last time and waited for Veniamin at the top of the cliff. Already I had bid St. Anthimus' penitentiary cave a second farewell.

About eight o'clock (I say *about* eight — the loss of my watch has made me very time conscious), I heard Veniamin approaching. He was singing in his squeaky old voice as loud as a herd of thirsty elephants trumpeting for water. When he saw me he ran — galloped — to me, grabbed my hands and pulled me off the ground, hugged me, kissed me and shouted, "A miracle has come! God has given me a miracle on my birthday today! Oh blessed morning!"

He held up his arm. On his wrist was my watch.

"I found it by the Lavra path spring. Is it not beautiful?" he said, "Beautiful! Beautiful!" He crossed himself. "Thank you, God, for my beautiful watch."

My guts churned and little demons ran around the inside of my skull and tempted me; and then I thought of the carving on the wall of my new cave: GENTLE LORD, I THANK THEE FOR THY ENDLESS BOUNTY. I put my arms around Veniamin. "God's rewarded you for your love. You've deserved that watch for many years." I couldn't think of anything else to say, so I hugged him.

"Now," he said, "how are you? Let me look at you, dear brother."

He saw my rash. Putting his finger on my skin, he said, "Oh, so you have the saint's ailment. It's the evils oozing out of you. A good omen. I had it also when I fasted. Now tell me, dear brother, how are you? I want to know how you are this very moment," he said moving his wrist with a great flourish and looking at the watch, "at this moment, which is exactly twenty-one minutes until nine on my birthday morning."

I told him I was very happy because God had given him a beautiful watch and that I also was happy because God had done a miracle for me too. He had led me to a wonderful new cave that was warm and comfortable and beautiful — that I'd been cold and miserable and frightened with St. Anthimus. Veniamin asked me where it was, and I told him. He asked for details, and when I told him it was in an amphitheater made of concave, smooth rock, he opened his mouth, pulled on his beard a few times while he stared at the ground. He raised his head, looked directly at me and asked me if I had heard any strange noises near the cave.

I told him about the moaning and screaming and was about to tell him the whole story when he wailed, "Sweet Mother of Jesus protect us! The Cave of the Demons! Thank God I've come this morning. Stay away from there, for God's sake. For over a thousand years everyone who's gone to that cave has been eaten by the demons, with one exception — the Holy Skopias. Only Skopias conquered them. He lived there for eighteen years. The demons were his slaves. But when he left, the demons got their power back."

I tried to interrupt him to tell him what had happened, but he kept on babbling, his face tense with frenzy and fear.

"During the war, a monk took St. Anne's cross to the Cave of the Demons, thinking it would be a safe place to hide it from the Germans. He didn't return. We went to look for him. He was dead near the front of the cave, clutching the cross. The demons had killed him, but because of the cross they couldn't eat him. We returned there the next day with crosses and with lighted candles and singing hymns — and just as we got near the body, the demons started screaming and shouting and blew out the candles with their foul breaths. But we got the body back and the monk today is buried at St. Anne's. No one but Skopias has ever come out of that cave alive."

He stopped for a moment to catch his breath, and I said, "I put stones in the throats of the demons and quieted them. . . ."

"*You did what?*"

Again I started to tell him, and again he interrupted, babbling hysterically, telling me of one monk after another who'd been a victim of the demons. Only last year a monk tried to go into the cave. The demons screamed at him, entered his body, and he ran all the way back to this very spot and jumped off the cliff.

He sat down, moaned, and put his head between his hands.

"Listen to me," I said. "There are no more demons. Come with me. I'll show you." He turned pale and pulled on his beard again. "Come," I said, "I'll show you there are no more demons. God's done many miracles lately."

"No," he said. "And the abbot must know about this."

I said, "I swear to Jesus I'm telling the truth. There are no demons. You won't be harmed, I swear to God."

I picked up my sleeping bag and started walking. On the way to "the Cave of the Demons" Veniamin followed me reluctantly, frequently falling behind; and when I stopped and waited for him he babbled more about the cave, repeating himself often. His normally slow speech was hurried, agitated, his breathing constricted.

"Only one person in a thousand years has conquered the demons — Skopias the mason. . . ."

"Skopias the what?"

"The mason. Skopias was a famous sculptor-priest. He got into trouble by saying that all people are equal because we're all created in God's image. Kings and beggars are the same. This angered the emperor. Skopias further said that dogma means nothing — it is the dung of dead people and should not be believed. One should only believe his own experiences. This angered the patriarchs. The soldiers were sent after Skopias; but he escaped in a small boat and sailed to the Holy Mountain alone, landing where New Skete is. He went to the Cave of the Demons and performed the miracle of conquering them. Many other priests have tried. The demons have either eaten them or entered their bodies and they went crazy." Veniamin sat down and said, "Let us rest for a while."

After several minutes he said, "Giorgho, I don't want to die on my seventy-third birthday." He looked up at me, "You were actually in the cave?"

"Yes."

"What did the demons look like?"

"There are no demons. You will see. The cave is beautiful and I'm going to live there."

"Perhaps Satan quieted them so that you'd bring me and the demons could have my blood as well as yours?"

"When we get there, I'll go in first," I said. "There are no demons. You can stand outside and watch."

He stood up. "On this whole peninsula, there are only two spots the monks fear: the Cave of the Demons and the Cave of the Living Dead. Giorgho, I'm frightened."

I told him that there was no danger and, anyway, today was his day of miracles and nothing could harm him.

When we got to the cave, the moaning and screaming was loud and fierce. We stood at the far side of the field listening, Veniamin trembling. He looked at me accusingly and said, "You swore to Jesus that there were no more demons."

"I told the truth."

"Then what in hell is the shrieking? It's not the abbot saying mass."

"If I told you you'd think I'm crazy. But it's not demons. It's God.

And I'll show you. You watch. Stay right here while I go in."

I walked the several hundred feet to the cave entrance. Before I entered, I turned and waved. Veniamin was on his knees, his hands stretched imploringly to heaven. I went in. The noise was so loud I held my hands over my ears — and almost had to push against the thunder as if I were leaning into a gale. I reached the far end and shoved the big stone into place, then the small one. Then came the blessed silence. I left the cave and walked across the field to where Veniamin still was on his knees. I told him I'd made the screaming stop. Now I'd go back and start it again, and then I'd stop it again.

I did this. I came out and shouted to him that now I'd start the deep moaning only. I'd stop that and then start the shrill screaming. And then I'd stop that.

I did all this and then joined Veniamin on the field. He now was standing up and appeared somewhat relieved; although I guesses he still was suspicious of me. I took his hand and said that we'd go into the cave together and he'd soon learn that the noises were God-made, not demons.

He mumbled prayers and fingered the crucifix around his neck as we entered and kept staring at me as if perhaps I was in league with Satan and if, at any moment, I might sprout horns and turn into a demon. I let loose his hand and gave him the flashlight to hold. He moved the beam in every direction as we moved ahead.

When we got to the holes, I carefully explained the phenomenon that made the noises. I had to go over it several times before he said he understood. Then, warning him what would happen, I lifted the smaller stone — and the moment the high-pitched shriek started, Veniamin leaped back. I dropped the small stone back over the hole — and there was silence. I did this twice more and then had him do it. We did the same thing on the big stone, lifting and moving it together. I cracked the space over the small hole just a little, and when I felt no breeze, I removed both of the stones. Then I told Veniamin to tell me what sounds he heard coming from way deep in the passages.

"Waves," he said. "Waves beating against the cliffs."

Now he understood and was convinced. He smiled, a smile of great discovery and said quietly, "It is true. God and Satan have the same voice."

We went back out into the sunlight; and when we got there, a now jovial Veniamin said, "Giorgho, my brother in miracles, is there any raki left?"

I told him almost a full bottle.

"Then let us drink to our miracles and to my birthday. Let us celebrate."

I told him I was still fasting and that he could drink for both of us. I found the cup and the raki and poured enough for two, and gave him the cup. Veniamin poured water from my flask into the cooking pot, put about a teaspoonful of raki into it and handed it to me, and said, "When there are two miracles in one day and it also is my birthday, then I cannot drink alone."

We toasted the miracles, each other, Skopias the Mason, and God. Veniamin refilled the cup and said, "And a toast to Satan because Satan and God are one." After he had drunk, he grinned and said, "You stay outside. I'd like to take the stones off by myself and then put them back myself when the noise starts. But, oh yes, give me the flashlight first."

In about an hour, Veniamin said he had to get back to St. Anne's. As he turned to go, he placed his forefinger over his lips and said, "It is best that we tell no one about this. The monks cherish the thought of a cave of demons. If they learn that there is no evil, they'll be very unhappy."

He looked very relieved when I agreed. He glanced at his watch, said, "Yes, I better go now. On the way back I'll need time to pray and meditate — to calm myself — or they'll start asking questions." He looked at his watch again, smiled at it lovingly. "You darling, you! You'll get me back in time for dinner." He clapped me on the back and said he'd see me in two weeks.

SUNDAY, 15 OCTOBER 1967

SKOPIAS' CAVE

~~~~~~~~~~~~~~~~~~

My fasting period is more than half over. The last seven days (since I moved here) have been so pleasant, so productive that I regret I'll be breaking my fast in nineteen days. I'd like my present condition to go on and on. However I know that forty days is the approximate physical limit. After that the body consumes muscle tissue and organs — in short, starvation begins. Before that the body nourishes itself with nonessential material such as excess fat. It also consumes ailing or degenerate tissues. To make them usable, the body first disposes of filth and toxins — hence the rashes, coated tongue and continued bowel movements. There is a specific word for this self-regulation and self-purification process; but I cannot recall it. Note: I've had no food for twenty-one days — only water — and I still have small daily bowel movements.

However I believe I'm about cleaned out. My rash is gone. My skin is smoother and clearer than I remember it ever being; and my tongue now is pink again and I have a good, sweet taste in my mouth.

The last week has been euphoric. It contrasts to my stay at St. Anthimus' Cave where I was cold, tense, frightened, apprehensive; and even though I had some marvelously positive experiences there, I did not "enter the light." Instructions for fasting should emphasize that it be done only in an environment of physical, mental, emotional comfort, peace, safety, and love. This may be what's meant by "in the wilderness." There certainly should be no distractions. The cave of Skopias the Mason is the proper environment. Here my body can relax, rest, and cleanse and recreate itself. The energies usually used in everyday activities, in some mysterious way, now activate my unconscious repositories and spiritual reservoirs. I now understand how it is that many religious revelations — for example, those of Jesus, Moses, Buddha, Mohammed, Lao-tse and various saints — came after "fasting in the wilderness for forty days." However, the revelations, I believe came from within the prophets and saints themselves — not from an outside supernatural source. Every one of us has the same spiritual and consciousness inventory; but most of us need the "forty days" (or a similar experience) to eliminate our previous social conditioning and tap our vast and beautiful insides.

It is important to consider this. The great religious and philosophical leaders may have had revelations that *appeared* to come from outside forces, but I am convinced that the actual revelations, the perceptions, came from within themselves; and these revelations concerned individual man's relations with other people, creatures, things, energies, and also with himself. Add these up and you get élan vital: some call it God.

The relationships and behaviors that result in individual and collective well-being, these generally are called God's commandments — regardless of their origin. Buddha, perhaps, explained the commandments more clearly and in more detail than did other recorded leaders. The commandments sum up the behaviors that make it possible to cope gracefully with the inevitable, the inexorable, the inescapable problems and hardships and sufferings that are inherent in life. There is the violence of birth, the misery of sickness, and the necessity of earning shelter, food, and clothing. There are the ravages of time, which ultimately destroy whatever we acquire or build. There are floods, plagues, wars, typhoons, tidal waves, and other natural disasters. There are human beings who are negative and hostile. There are disappointments, failures, the loss of loved ones. And in the end, there is death itself. God's commandments are those behaviors and attitudes that make it possible to cope with life's endless problems gracefully and lovingly; and to view the hardships and sufferings as factors with which we can joyfully be consonant. God's commandments tell us how to live in concord, not discord, how to create heaven on earth.

Heraclitus spells these principles out. Sheila defined them beautifully in her letter. How do they apply? In my present environment and condition, I can see clearly how in the past I've violated law after law, and that's what almost destroyed me. I am not blaming myself or feeling guilty. That's how it was; and my only course is to try to improve. I have to get rid of the survival tactics I used at the orphanage. In those hectic days, I had to perform better than anyone else — so much better that everyone admitted it. I was so frightened and lonely that I had to feel superior even when I knew I was not. My whole nervous system developed to allow me to survive emotionally as a small boy in what seemed to be a hostile environment. As I grew older, those survival tactics no longer were needed. But by then they had become habits that needed feeding; and so I continually created negative survival conditions to accomodate the anachronistic nervous system. That's how I related to people. Poor Sheila! I often cunningly — yet without being aware of it — provoked her to attack me. And then blamed her.

The question is, will I be able to maintain my clearer thinking and my active desire for harmony after I return to normal society? I believe it is possible if I can but remember. Perhaps, like Bishop Andrew, I'll have to fast for four or five weeks annually to maintain my health and awareness.

SATURDAY, 21 OCTOBER 1967
SKOPIAS' CAVE

~~~~~~~~~~~~~~~~~~~~~~~~~~

T he last three days have been among the most peaceful — and yet most active — days of my entire life. The fasting has cleared my mind and senses. The aloneness has eliminated many distractions and has given my brain and senses the opportunity to explore new worlds. I hear the songs of birds, the whir of insects, the rustling of leaves, the love song of the wind caressing the earth. I see auras of vitality in all things. I smell and touch things I never knew existed. The energy within the cave glows; and it bathes me. My body feels light and comfortable. My mind dances through metaphysics. I visualize God not as an anthropomorphic power in the sky, a thing that looks like a biblical patriarch, but as an all-inclusive energy — an energy with absolute intelligence and laws. I have called it élan vital. At the same time, I wonder how it is that men are so erratic. Some are good. Some are evil. Some are both. How is this possible? After all, "Let us make man in our image, after our likeness." Is God, too, both good and evil? And if there is a God, we should be able to define and predict it, as we can almost all other natural phenomena.

While I wondered at and was troubled by these thoughts, I saw a man climbing down the steep hill, coming in the direction of the cave. My inclination was to remove the two rocks and have the moaning and shrieking frighten the intruder away. That may be the way Skopias the Mason preserved his privacy. While considering this, I recognized the huge hulk of the man. It was Alexis. I was not surprised to see him. Somehow I'd had the feeling that we hadn't separated after Gythion.

I asked Alexis how he had found me. He said he had gone to St. Anthimus' Cave and, not seeing signs of me, had begun looking around. He had noticed the trail of notched trees and followed it here.

I looked him over, "You're a monk again?"

"Not yet," he said, grinning slyly and chuckling in his deep voice, "I put the monk's clothes back on to get here and see you. And, Giorgho, you look as thin and joyful as a saint. But I know you're not a saint and never will be." He slapped me on the back, laughing, and said, "And how are you? You look like an icon — your bones sticking out, sunburned, with a wild white beard, — and I see you've learned to roll your eyes toward heaven as if you're the only one in the world who can see angels and God. The environment's certainly influenced you!"

He told me he'd spent the last month just thinking; but that he couldn't test his conclusions until he'd lived among ordinary people — not in a monastery or isolated on a mountaintop. And then, once more, he asked me about myself?

I told him everything was going well, but there was one thing that I simply couldn't understand or figure out. If we human beings are made in the image of God, then why are most of us greedy, vain, filled with discord, and in bad health both physically and spiritually? Is God, in whose image we're supposedly made, in the same miserable and inconsistent state?

Alexis said, "Are we — God and Man — not of the same stuff? If we're greedy and vain and arrogant, then so is God. If we're joyful, serene, and conscious, then so is God. As we change, so does God. And as for our having pain, physical sickness and daily problems — this is common to all living things. We are all born, struggle every day of our lives, and die. So does God. We are immortal only through our children — it is a genetic immortality. Likewise, God is immortal only through God's children. We are God's children. It's simple, Giorgho. If we think and behave with love — and stay aware, awake and responsive — then so does God. If we fail to do this, we already are dead. And, likewise, so is God. There are no further mysteries."

I then pointed out the mystery of my trip. Everything, it seems, had happened by "mysterious accident": the book contract came unexpectedly; the Greece trip came unexpectedly; *Varvaros* was unexpected; and so were Gregory, Ziggy, Maria, Ito, the bishop, Constantine, Veniamin, and Alexis. Each of these people served a specific function in shaping my trip — which turned out to be a physical, psychological, and spiritual adventure; and the psychological and spiritual may well turn out to be the most influential and manifest. The literary project now appears to have been incidental.

Certainly such a sequence of unusual events — none of them planned or created by me — doesn't usually happen by accident. If not by accident, then how and by what energy had such a complex sequence been arranged?

"You've already answered both questions in one of your books*," said Alexis. "I'll retell part of your tale to remind you — with a few variations."

Alexis told the story slowly, walking back and forth, continually gesticulating, often pausing to think, sometimes intoning as if in mass.

"Nature, the infinite energy," said Alexis, speaking in Greek, "creates spontaneously. Man had to have a concept and he called it God. God creates spontaneously, not by plan. When God has an idea, the idea becomes a reality. If God imagines, say, a macadamia tree, then a macadamia tree becomes a reality. If there were no such things as

God Needs Man.

elephants and God thought about creatures that looked like elephants, elephants would become realities. And so it has been with all things — whales, planets, universes, bedbugs, and the paramecium. God has but to think of them and they become.

"However once a creature, a tree — whatever it is — is created, from that moment on, it's on its own. If there's to be a change, the creature or thing must do the changing by itself. And if one changes, so must all others adjust. The cosmos is a system that stays in balance. All the entities of the universe were developed as incremental gods, who must stay in balance with each other and change themselves, adapt, continually. God stays out of the changing process. That's why any prayer except one of thanks is absurd. Besides, God is very busy. God is involved in a problem of God's own. What's the problem — the one that up to now God has been unable to solve? The problems is this: God is everything and therefore God can't define God. That's why God needs man. It is only man who can — by his consciousness — let God know what God is. Without our consciousness, God has no identity and is therefore unable to verify God's own existence. God can do anything — with one exception. God cannot create God. That's why God needs man."

Alexis paused at this point, scratched his head in thought, and quoted a short passage from my book:

> The endlessness of Me
> is endless. And so,
> I can't perceive Myself.
> The whole's not privy
> to itself;
> it has no outside point
> from which to stand away
> and see.
> And so I'm naught.
>
> I willed, I'll not be naught.
> That which I want,
> that thing I make.

I spread myself
and it is done.

We mixed the juices of ourselves
with fertile earth
and formed our children such
as we would like to be
and thus gave birth to man,
female and male.

It was our anxious wish
to dialogue with man,
so We could understand ourselves
and know what We are like.

"You remember that?" asked Alexis. I nodded.

He continued narrating:

"Yes, God begat man — God-children — so that they could stand off in their full consciousness, see God and tell God what It was like. And God was pleased; and ordered all creatures of the earth to gather, bend their knees in homage to God, and worship. All creatures obeyed, except the God-children, female and male. They refused, saying that they were made in God's image and were, therefore, God's equal.

"God thundered and scolded — but God's own breath — the Word transformed to flesh, men and women — refused to kneel and worship. So God became angry and threw them out. As they departed, they laughed at God — their father and mother — and said, 'Silly God, now you'll never know who you are or what you're like

"God lost Its temper and omniscience; and in a rage caused countless seeds to fall upon the earth; and pronounced that from these seeds would grow beast-men and weed-men, female and male. In every way they physically would resemble the God-men, but they would have no God-consciousness. Instead, they would be filled with evil, greed, hate; and they would kill, steal, lie, cheat; and they would multiply like weeds and would choke out the few ungrateful God-men.

"And all this came to pass, except the God-men were not choked out. They hid and camouflaged themselves so well that it was impossible to tell the beast-men from the God-men. And it came to pass that the earth became a turmoil of war, murder, hate, greed, and pestilence.

"Then God regained omniscience and wanted the God-children back. But so skillfully had God wrought, that God could not identify God's own children. God yearned for them; and knew there was only one way to have them return.

"The only way to have the God-men back was to raise all human beings up to the level of God-men. But God could not do this. If the beast-men were to change, they had to do it alone and voluntarily.

"And so God whispered into the ears of those whom God hoped might hear the silent voice; and God requested them to go forth among the beast-men and tell of the glories of raising themselves up to the God-level.

"Jesus, Moses, Isaiah, Gautama, Lao-tse, and a hundred others received the Word; and they passed it on. A few heard and tried to change, but not many. The world still turmoiled with war, greed, murder, and other evils.

"God has made many attempts, and always has failed. Yet God keeps trying. God knows that until all men obey God's commandments and have God-consciousness, God will "be naught." And so God's silent voice still tries to reach the inner ears. God still needs man to find out who God is and what God is like."

When Alexis finished the story, it was almost dawn. He went to the back of the cave and lay down. I stayed up, thinking. Shortly after the sun rose, I heard a donkey bray. I looked out. Coming down the hill on a donkey was a monk. It was Veniamin. I wasn't expecting him. He wasn't supposed to come and check on me until my twenty-eighth day — tomorrow. Veniamin waved a piece of paper and shouted. He was too far away for me to hear. But he kept waving the paper.

The donkey reached the bottom of the hill and I heard the clop clop clop of his hooves. When Veniamin was about two hundred yards away he waved the paper and shouted again, "Giorgho! A letter for you! Very urgent!"

Veniamin rode up, slid off the donkey, thrust the envelope at me, "Urgent! I'm to wait for the answer. The messenger from Athens has orders to hand this to you personally and bring back your answer. But I wouldn't let him come here; and I promised to do it for him."

The letter was from Agios.

> Dear Giorgho,
>
> Sheila telephoned. Your stepmother, Mimi, is dying. She wants to see you ("my son, the only person I've ever loved") before she dies. The doctor has verified that she's in a bad way and that she is calling for you. She may hang on a month if she knows you'll be there. I have the doctor's number and I'm to call and inform him whether or not you'll do it. The messenger will wait for your reply. If the answer is yes, give me instructions. I'll arrange your flight.
>
> Agios

I read the letter several times. Veniamin was impatient and nagged me for an answer. I told him, weakly, wearily, "I have to think. I didn't sleep last night and my head's not working well."

"What will I tell the messenger?" said Veniamin.

"Tell him I'll have a reply by tomorrow."

"He may not believe me. Can you write him a note and sign your name on it? I'll give him your note and then come back again tomorrow."

I wrote the note. I thanked Veniamin for all his help and generosity and requested that he return tomorrow afternoon. "Not in the morning," I said. "I need time to think."

I went to sleep. When I awakened at noon, Alexis was up, munching the crunchy bread that Veniamin had brought almost a month ago.

"Well?" he said.

"Well, what?"

"You left your letter out and I read it. Are you going?"

I was silent for about five minutes, and Alexis didn't press me. Then I said, "Alexis, for fifty-one years I've hated Mimi. She's my stepmother. Hold that fact in your left hand. In your right hand, consider how happy I am here in this cave. I've been determined to go through the same process most saints have gone through before they had their illumination — fasting in the wilderness for forty days. I have only two weeks more. I'm weak, and I am beginning to crave food, and my body is ready. My tongue is pink. My mouth is fresh. I probably am approaching my spiritual illumination, my nirvana.

In short, I like what's happening here — and I don't like Mimi. I owe her nothing. Not a goddam thing! But I have to think about it."

"When you die," said Alexis, "do you want to die alone?"

"No. But I want someone with me whom I love and who loves me."

"From the letter, it appears that Mimi loves you and must think you love her. And if she but *thinks* it, for a dying person it's very real."

"Mimi's never loved anyone in her life. She's just scared. Or maybe just faking."

Alexis swallowed the bread he had been chewing, walked over to me and placed his big hand on my shoulder, "You're also scared. You're scared you won't be able to say that you fasted in the wilderness for the full forty days the way Moses, Jesus, Buddha, and all the great saints did. Perhaps you're scared you'll be looked at as weak and then your ego and vanity will take a bashing. On top of that, it's possible that *you're* faking."

"Faking? How?"

"About the God and saint business."

I began thinking about this, but before I reached a conclusion, Alexis continued: "Giorgho, do you know the difference between eros and caris?"

"Yes."

"What is it?"

"Eros is a form of love that is like what an infant has, and it expresses 'give me what I need and I'll behave the way you want.' Caris is when you give and want nothing back, not even satisfaction — when you give because it's the right and loving thing to do; and therefore there's no alternative if you're a spiritual individual."

Alexis squeezed my shoulder and said, "Giorgho, if you loved Mimi and she loved you, you'd get pleasure from helping her die in peace. You'd get satisfaction. That's pure eros, isn't it? Any pharisee can do that. But what is it if you love your enemy and get nothing back? Especially if you make your enemy happy — even if the enemy is faking, is lying. If you help your enemy die happy and in peace — even if it defeats your ambition to fast here for another two weeks and also defeats the possibility that you'll get a saint's illumination — what is that? Come, Giorgho, what is that?"

"Caris."

"Is it possible that caris is what your saints learned during their six weeks of fasting? And is it possible that some people might learn about caris in four weeks instead of six? Think about that for a little."

We discussed the subject all afternoon; and as we talked I knew I hadn't progressed much during my month of fasting. I still had negative thoughts about Mimi, my father, my mother, Sheila, and perhaps a dozen others; and these negative thoughts stampeded around my skull, and I couldn't stop them. The best I could do was to stand back and observe them and hope I could let them pass by and not influence my behavior and decisions. By wrestling them, I was feeding them.

During my "saint's interval" I had cleansed my alimentary canal and the rest of my body, but I hadn't succeeded in washing out the psychological poisons that had accumulated in my mind over a half-century. Sure, I'd been filled with beautiful thoughts and had soared on spiritual flights during my month's stay on Mount Athos. But to harvest this effort I had to behave and think NOW (not in the future sometime or in the dead past) with caris, with love — even if I had to force myself to do it mechanically, the same way I had done when I made love to Ito. And I tensed when I realized that after the first time, I had been able to make love authentically.

And behaving with caris and love — I had to do this among people in the real world. Doing it when alone in an ivory tower is easy. But if I couldn't make myself do it in the real world of people — people as weak and faultful as I am, whether I believe them or not, whether I love them or not — then my entire Greek adventure would be a fraud.

We talked about this until late at night. I know I would not have had the courage to explore the subject honestly without Alexis' help.

SUNDAY, 22 OCTOBER 1967

SKOPIAS' CAVE

~~~~~~~~~~~~~~~~~~~~~~

In the morning when I awakened, Alexis was gone. He hadn't even left a note.

But I had made three decisions: (1) I'd go to Mimi; (2) I would continue my fast, even in America; (3) I would return here after I had comforted Mimi and stay here until the forty days were over.

Veniamin came back around one. I gave him a note for Agios, requesting Agios to get me space on a flight leaving Athens on Wednesday.

I asked Veniamin to come back for me tomorrow, and could he bring a donkey? I was too weak to travel the rough mountains on my own. And please tell the abbot that I'd leave New Skete by motorboat — for Ouranopolis and then to Athens.

TUESDAY, 24 OCTOBER 1967

ATHENS

~~~~~~~~~~~~~~~~~~~~~~~~~~~~~~~~~~~~~

I took the bus from Ouranopolis to Thessaloniki, and from there flew to Athens. Maria and Agios met the plane. Maria hugged me and with happy laughter told me my clothes hung on me like a scarecrow's. Agios said that before I had new clothes and a haircut, he wanted me to meet the press. They would be impressed with how I had duplicated the fasting ordeal of the saints about whom I had written; and the publicity would give the book a stamp of authenticity. I refused. I said I wasn't up to meeting the press. Further, the event had been private and personal. Agios grumbled, saying that my gauntness gave me a saintly look; and that if I met the press after publication, I'd probably be fat again. But I refused again, and Agios did not insist.

I weighed myself. 139 pounds. That is skinny! Both Agios and Maria praised me again and again. Later, at Agios' house, he called in a woman photographer and said it was necessary to have a photograph of me with my long hair and a month's beard, unkempt and untrimmed. He wanted it for the book's jacket. Once more I refused.

However, later, when I was alone with Maria, she took a picture of me to show her uncle. Then we went to the barber and to buy clothes suitable for the trip. Maria asked about my adventure. I told her I'd rather not talk about it. She nodded and said she understood.

WEDNESDAY, 25 OCTOBER 1967
FLIGHT TO N.Y.

~~~~~~~~~~~~~~~~~~~~~~~~

I'm on the plane to New York. The noise and bustle jar me. Also, I'm nervous. I dread seeing Mimi. I already can hear her criticizing me the moment I arrive. "Why didn't you come sooner? You know I'm deathly sick. I've always loved you, you know that, darling."

Suppose she dies while I'm there?

I am trying to change those negative thoughts to positive ones. I cannot do it. So, instead, I'm sitting back and observing the thoughts as they run through my brain. By simply observing them, I don't let them become part of me. It's like being at a motion picture show. In that way, I don't feed them.

If it hadn't been for Alexis, I would not have had the courage to start this trip. But even now I have only the courage to do what I *must* do, not what I want to do.

Mimi's probably not dying at all. Mimi's a great actress. Even when she was young and beautiful, she'd pretend to be ill if she needed that ploy to get what she wanted. She'll probably live for years — her mother lived to be 96 — and as soon as she feels better, she'll ask me to stay with her for months.

My thoughts are destructively negative. I better try to remember the loving counsel Alexis gave me. Caris! Caris! Caris! Oh, I still have a long way to go. Probably I'll never make it.

I had told the stewardess I didn't want any meals; but she brought me a bowl of fruit — beautiful apples, bananas, pears. That's the food one has for breaking fasts. Fresh fruit. My salivary glands started squirting; and I imagined myself having half an apple, chewing it slowly. It tasted very good. I thought, Why not?

Why not? I haven't eaten anything for thirty-one days. My tongue is pink and my skin is clear. I've had a few spiritual experiences. Doesn't that mean I can break my fast? Also, I'm under great strain — no longer in the peace and quiet of my cave on Mount Athos. Why not have some food nourishment? How else can I get the strength to survive my experiences with Mimi? And all the rushing around and physicality of New York. Yes, I needed some calories to see me through. I thought I saw Gregory sitting on the other side of the aisle, grinning at me and saying, "Come now, one doesn't live by bread alone."

I thought, George, what a precious fraud you are — trying to play that phony messiah bit! I smiled to myself and thought, Is it fasting for forty days in the wilderness that I want? Well, I'm in the real wilderness now, and the most dangerous jungle is coming up. The next few days are the real test! Across the aisle, Gregory held up two fingers in the victory sign. No, it was Alexis.

WEDNESDAY, 25 OCTOBER 1967
AT NEW YORK AIRPORT

I am waiting for my rented car. It's almost 5 P.M., and it's about a four-hour drive to Orford, perhaps six hours what with the rush-hour traffic. I'm afraid to drive in the heavy traffic because I'm weak, low in energy, and my whole system's still geared to the peace of Mount Athos. I shouldn't go to Orford now. I should get a good night's sleep to prepare myself. I'm still on Greek time. Maybe I should stay in New York for a few days and acclimate and rest?

THURSDAY, 26 OCTOBER 1967
NEW YORK
THIRTY-THIRD DAY OF FAST

~~~~~~~~~~~~~~~~~~~~~~~~~~~~~

I stayed overnight near the airport. It's now 9:30. I'm eating "breakfast" in my room. A big bottle of Perrier and the *New York Times.*

I telephoned Mimi and spoke to dear old Mary (Mimi's still asleep); and I told Mary I'd be there mid-afternoon. God, I'm glad Mary's still alive! She must be eighty. She was the servant (slave) when I arrived there as a little boy. Oh, that beautiful, tall, skinny African — black as midnight — the only person in Orford whom I trusted and who always was kind to me, even when I was bad. Everyone treated her like dirt, and I've never understood why she's spent her life there. She and Mimi are the only ones left — Mary's been there sixty years.

Mary confirmed that Mimi's been hanging on just to see me and is frantically, desperately, looking forward to my arrival. "It's a good idea not getting here 'til this afternoon," she said. "Mimi's having someone from the beauty parlor come this morning to doll her up."

THURSDAY, 26 OCTOBER 1967
ENROUTE NEW YORK TO ORFORD

~~~~~~~~~~~~~~~~~~~~~~~~~~~~~~~~

I t's 3:10. I've gotten lost several times on a route I know well. Is six-year-old George trying to stop me from going to Mimi's?

About fifteen miles from Orford, I got a stomachache. Soon after that I felt the same old dull pain in my chest, and twinges in my left arm. I drove very, very slowly, watching other cars carefully, concentrating on being alert. I noticed how tightly my hands held the wheel and how I hunched over it. Several times I pulled over, got out of the car, shook my hands loosely in the effort to relax them, massaged my eyes, took deep breaths.

I thought, What in hell is happening?

I analyzed the situation as best I could. It's true, I thought, what Buddha told us: everything's controlled by what's happening in our heads. Okay, take a look. I *am* low in physical energy, but my reflexes are superb and I'm alert. I'm actually driving better now than usual because I'm driving consciously, not automatically. Then why are there pains in my heart and stomach? I'll tell you why. Those pains and aches are in my head, not in my body. My body's learned discipline and courage and honesty. But my head's still fearful and looking for excuses, and trying to fabricate hardships so that I can kid myself that I'm a martyr or a hero.

One unpleasant memory after another assaulted me as I drove closer and closer to the square stone house where I had lived for eight years. Mimi's family's house — where I had been treated like an orphan. Then I saw the house up on the hill, surrounded by pine trees. Had I been in my right mind, I would have gotten pleasure from the beauty of the scene. Instead, I remembered that it had been my job — at seven years old — to lug endless buckets of water from the spring at the bottom of the hill all the way to the house. There had to be water enough for nine people. On Monday, wash day, carrying water was an all-day chore.

I began to feel sorry for myself. Then the Gregory in me spoke up, "Look, you stupid bastard, whatever happens, it's there for you to milk. Whatever happens, squeeze some advantage out of it." Then I said aloud, "Perhaps those eight years of hell were a blessing. Life at Orford taught me how to hustle and survive." I didn't really believe it, but that's what I told myself.

I stopped at the bottom of the hill and sat there quietly for a few minutes, composing myself, reminding myself that unless I could maintain the attitudes I had experienced in my cave on Mount Athos, then my entire Greek experience was a waste, an obscenity, a counterfeit.

THURSDAY, 26 OCTOBER 1967
ORFORD

~~~~~~~~~~~~~~~~~~~~~~~~~~~~~~~~~~

I drove up to the house and got out of the car. I heard Mary shout, "Mimi, he's here! He's here!"

The front door opened and Mimi very slowly stepped out, supporting herself on two canes. When she saw me, she dropped the canes inside and held herself erect, as if she didn't need them. She *was* dolled up. Her hair was black (the last time I'd seen her it had been gray), and she wore the silk kimono I'd impulsively sent her from Japan when I was in the navy. From ten feet away, what with the carefully applied makeup, her face looked young; and, at that moment, her resemblance to Sheila shocked me.

"Darling! Darling!" she shouted. "Where in the hell have you been? Oh, my darling! I've waited so long for this."

Her voice had the same throatiness, the same demanding quality I had associated with her for the last half-century. It sounded just the way it had sounded on my birthday in 1916, when she had said, "We must find a home for this boy. We'll send him to my family in Orford. It will be good for him." That was the same day she had fired

Ilya. It was the same day she went off traveling with Papa. I remember the results of that throaty, demanding voice only too well. While Mimi and Papa were traipsing all over, I, now an orphan, was stuck in Orford with a big, noisy, hostile family. Although I had a father and stepmother, the reality, for me, was that the place was an orphanage. All of them, except Mary, harrassed me, abused me, made fun of me. I hated them. But I survived for eight years by withdrawing and hiding my emotions, by acting superior, by forcing myself to hustle and accomplish things that they could not. The terrible ruthlessness and ambition that years later had driven me to become a successful author probably had originated in my desire to outshine those eight other "siblings" at Orford.

Mimi shouted, "George! I haven't seen you for twenty years. George, come over to me!"

I wanted to flee. I wanted to get back into the car, drive to the airport, and fly back to the peace and security of my cave on Mount Athos. But I heard Gregory speak sharply, "Resist the temptation. This is the hardest one of all." And I heard Alexis softly say, "Caris! Caris!" And Ziggy, "This is a dying woman who wants assurance that her son, you, loves her. It's such a precious gift, George, give it to her."

I pushed my lips together hard and breathed deeply. I smiled as best I could, opened my arms, rushed over to her, hugged her, and, for a moment, lifted her off the ground. She kissed me wetly. Turning her head, she shouted, "Mary, bring my chair!"

Mary pushed a wheelchair out; and with a sigh, Mimi sank into it. Good old Mary! Eighty, still six feet of skinniness, black as midnight — with white hair knotted on the back of her head — and grinning broadly. I started to walk around to the back of the chair to greet Mary, but Mimi's hand clutched my wrist and she pulled me away from Mary and down toward herself. She put her arms around my neck, kissed me again, and said, "Darling, where have you been so long? You surely know I'm dying?"

"I've been in Greece."

"What? Speak up!

Behind her, Mary said softly, "She's deaf as a doorknob. You'll have to shout."

I shouted, "I've been in Greece."

"What?"

I bellowed as loud as I could, "I've been in Greece."

"Why didn't you come to see my first?"

Mary took charge and wheeled the chair into the house — with Mimi still clutching my wrist. She tugged at me. "How do I look, darling?"

"You look wonderful."

"What? Can't you talk louder?"

"You look wonderful," I shouted, articulating carefully so that she might read my lips.

"Oh, darling, you never were able to tell the truth. Here I am deaf, almost blind, and dying — and you tell me I look wonderful. But I love every word of it! I love you, darling."

"I've brought you a present."

She looked up at me and shouted, "What? For God's sake, speak up."

I handed her the small box that the Ziggy in me had suggested I get yesterday in the hotel gift shop. It was a bottle of Mountain Flowers, Mimi's favorite perfume. She opened the package eagerly, almost by feel, tearing off the paper and ribbon. She removed the glass stopper, sniffed, made sounds of satisfaction, and dabbed the perfume behind her ears. She looked at me, smiling — in the same way that Sheila did when she was happy. "Oh, darling, you remembered. You do love me, don't you? You know how hard I worked to see that you were looked after and were brought up properly and learned good manners." Then she put her hands up to her face and began weeping, smudging her makeup.

Mary brought out a medicine bottle and fed Mimi two teaspoonsful. "Time to rest now," she said.

"What? Speak up, you imbecile!"

277

Mary shouted close to Mimi's ear, "Time for you to rest, dear."

Mimi threw her arms about my neck again and said loudly, "I have to sleep in the afternoon. See you at cocktails, darling." And then another kiss. I waved to her as Mary wheeled her away. She waved back with both hands, and blew me still another kiss. When she was out of sight, I sat down — I fell into the chair. I had been fasting for thirty-three days and was weak. I had been putting on an act that I loved someone whom I disliked and feared. I had felt weak many times before, but never like this. I had used up all my reserves. If true compassion had been pouring from me, perhaps I would have been renewed. What was blocking me? What was I doing wrong? In St. Anthimus' Cave, I had loved the stones, the trees, the spiders. Genuine warmth, affection, and joy had gushed from me. And now, here was a dying woman who needed and wanted to be loved, and I was unable to respond except as an actor. I groaned, and it seemed that my entire Greek experience was a failure.

Mary returned. Now that Mimi was not present, Mary seemed more relaxed. Her speech changed — as if she were speaking to me as a little boy again. She said, "Boy, that old woman sure loves you. She always love you . . . oh, my dear God, what that woman done for you and your daddy! She was like a saint." She sighed, "That Mimi sure do love you! She should have been dead months ago, but she been hangin' on just to see you, her son. She been hangin' on with so much pain an' hurt that doctor don' know how she stan' it."

I began weeping.

Mary said, "Hush now, boy, it make me cry too. But right now you better get some rest. You look mighty tired. Imagine not eatin' nothin' for over a month!" She put her arm around me and steered me in the direction of my room, and said, "Mimi sleep 'till 'bout seven. Then her martinis peps her up for 'bout an hour; and then when she drunk enough that nothing' hurtin' too much, she gets quick sponge bath an' goes to sleep. She be down 'bout seven, an' boy, no foolin', you be needin' rest. With them martinis in her, that

Mimi becomes a wild cat. Yes, sir, when she's feelin' no pain, she gets plenty wild. No tellin' what she want to do."

At cocktail time, Mim gulped one martini after another — and with each she filled my glass and shouted, "Bottoms up, old dear. I drink to the reunion with my loving son after all these years of his carousing all over the world and neglecting his old mother."

The first time this happened I told her I didn't drink anymore, and I reached for the water pitcher.

She said, "What? What?" and filled my glass.

Mary beckoned me to one side and said, "She don' see too well. Jus' dump the booze out. She never know difference. Thas' what I do."

In about half an hour Mimi was in a rollicking mood. I kept reminding myself, Behave as if you love her. Make her believe it. But already I was doing the best I could. And then I thought about Ito; and I went about my task with Mimi mechanically and with vigor. I laughed at Mimi's jokes. I hugged her. I held her hand. I behaved exactly as if I were courting her. But I felt nothing positive moving within me, except that I was trying my best, and I again wondered what was wrong with me. I had fasted, meditated, prayed for a month, alone in a cave in the wilds of Mount Athos — and nothing seemed to have changed in me.

Mimi told Mary to turn on the record player full blast — music of the twenties. She told me she wanted to dance and ordered me to hold her up so she could do the Charleston. I stood behind her and lifted her, my hands in her armpits. I was holding up about three-quarters of her weight. She laughed and began moving her legs and feet clumsily and pathetically in the Charleston.

"I haven't lost the old moxie, have I, darling?" Then she shouted at Mary to take my place in holding her up. When that was done, Mimi said, "C'mon, my best beau, this is our dance. C'mon, we'll burn up the floor."

What with Mary struggling to hold Mimi in a standing position, I stood opposite Mimi and did the Charleston with her. I worked hard trying to make it look like I was having a wonderful time; but I didn't love her and it was a painful experience, not one of joy. At that moment I remembered when I was in St. Anthimus' Cave and thought I might be dying. I had tried to figure out whom I'd want to be with me when I was dying, who would comfort me, who would make me smile during my last minutes of life. I had been unable to think of anyone, and it had grieved me. And here was Mimi, who truly was dying and who knew exactly whom she wanted with her to comfort her, to make her smile — me; and I wasn't able to do it from the heart.

Then, for a moment, I was back in the cave with Alexis and again I heard him say, "Giorgho, if you loved Mimi and she loved you, you'd get pleasure from helping her die in peace. You'd get satisfaction. That's pure eros, isn't it? Any pharisee can do that. But what is it if you love your enemy and get nothing back? Especially if you make your enemy happy — even if the enemy is faking, is lying. If you help your enemy be happy and in peace when she dies — even if it defeats your ambition to fast here for another two weeks and also defeats the possibility that you'll get a saint's illumination — what is that? Come, Giorgho, what is that?"

"Caris," I had said.

"Is it possible that caris is what your saints learned during their six weeks of fasting? And is it possible that some people might learn about caris in other ways — say, by acting with love when they don't feel the joys of love and when it is difficult to act with love?"

Mimi, still clumsily and weakly doing the Charleston, began singing the lyrics to the song; and I joined in at the top of my lungs.

"This is one hell of a party," Mimi said, panting hard. "This is one hell of a great party. Me and my kid making the Castles look like tramps. My God, I drew bigger crowds at the Palladium than they

did." Her breath came in gasps. Mary maneuvered her into the
wheelchair. She slumped and said wearily, "You've never seen my
clippings. They raved about that dance at the Palace. It always disappointed me that you never came to see me." She stared into space,
half smiling, perhaps recalling her many triumphs on the stage. Then
she looked around the room and shouted, "Mary, where the hell are
you?"

Mary went around to the front of the wheelchair, kneeled down,
and straightened Mimi's dress. Then she stood up hugged her, and
began wheeling her out, saying to me, "After her bath, she goes to
bed."

I went back to the dining room and sat down in the old morris
chair — the same one Mimi's mother had snoozed in every afternoon.
I thought; They're all dead — her father and mother, her brothers
and sisters. Only Mary and Mimi are still here. The same books stand
on the shelves. The same huge, battered oak table where a dozen of
us had eaten and bickered. I slowly went from room to room, recalling incidents that I had completely forgotten and that had occurred
in the various rooms. With every recollection, and every time I
exhaled, I choked, had spasms in my throat, and long-hidden emotions pushed out. As I coughed and disgorged them, I felt fresh air
and light rush into me. I could not explain it, but I had the same
sensation I had had when I moved from St. Anthimus' harsh cave
into the loving cave of Skopias. I had the feeling I was traveling from
the past anxieties of childhood into the realities of now.

From what seemed the distant upstairs, I heard Mimi screaming,
"George! George, my baby — where are you? George, come
here!"

Mary ran into the room. "Mimi won' keep quiet 'til you go there.
She look bad!"

I went to her bedroom, Mary behind me. The heat was stifling.
The two gas burners blazed. All the lights were on. Mimi lay in bed,
the covers half-down. Through her nightgown I saw the scars on the

right side of her chest where the cancerous breast had been removed. The other breast hung limply. Mimi's eyes were closed. She was murmuring, "Where's George? Where's my son?"

She looked terrible. Her black wig was askew, and her thin, white hair spilled out on one side. Her makeup was off. Her face was ashen, the skin mottled and rough with countless wrinkles. She looked very, very old. Softly, with great effort, she said, "George! George!"

I touched her. Her eyelids fluttered oepn, showing eyes that were dull and expressionless.

"You're here, my darling?"

I answered by squeezing her shoulder.

"What? What did you say?"

I put my head close to hers and shouted, "Yes, mother, I'm here."

"Thank God."

She closed her eyes and lay quiet for about a minute. Then she opened her eyes and said, "George, I'm cold."

I took her hands in mine.

"George! Did you hear me?"

I sat down on the bed, leaned over and embraced her. The decaying smell of age overpowered her perfume; and the touch of her cheek against mine was clammy.

"George, I'm very cold."

I lay down next to her on the bed and took her in my arms. She relaxed and hoarsely whispered, "George, do you love me?"

I lifted her head, kissed her on the mouth and I said, "Mother . . ."

"What?"

I kissed her again, then, very close to her, I said, "Mother I love you." And I caressed her with love and feeling. I did not need willpower or effort. It simply happened.

"I heard you," she said quietly, her wet wrinkled lips parting in a small smile. "And I feel you."

I held her tight. She lay still. My arm was uncomfortable and I moved it a little. Mimi said, "Don't go. Don't leave me!"

I continued holding her, saying nothing, my cheek next to hers. Then I heard her moan and felt her shudder. I raised my head and saw the saliva drooling from her still-smiling lips. I stayed there, holding her in my arms until Mary, sobbing, said that she was going to send for the doctor.

SATURDAY, 28 OCTOBER 1967

ORFORD

~~~~~~~~~~~~~~~~~~~~~~~~~~~~~~~~~~~~~

The mortician had done a good job. In her casket, Mimi looked young and pretty. She had the same happy smile that she had had two nights ago when I kissed her and told her I loved her.

While I was looking at Mimi — thinking how much she resembled Sheila — Mary came up and said, "Your Sheila's here for the funeral."

"What?"

"Sheila's here for the funeral."

I turned. There she was. She smiled shyly. I tried to smile, but I couldn't. I raised my hand and waved with my fingers; and then I walked to her, touched cheeks with her, and returned to the casket.

The undertaker came and said it was time to close the casket. I leaned over and kissed Mimi and said, "Mother, I love you." It was spontaneous. My heart filled. I kissed Mimi again and repeated, "Mother, I love you." As I did this I felt Alexis, Gregory, and Ziggy standing near me.

I felt Ziggy walk forward and stand next to me. No it was Sheila, tears sliding down her cheeks. She took my hand, and, while holding it, she also bent forward and kissed Mimi's cheek. Then, taking her hand from mine, she turned, walked across the room, and looked at herself in the mirror. Without drying her tears, she came back and took my hand again.

The undertaker screwed on the lid. Mary began sobbing. Sheila went to her and put her arm around her.

The raw grave was next to my father's grave. This was the first time I'd been here. His tombstone — which Mimi had put in — was plain. It simply had his name and the dates. Spilled all over his grave was fresh earth from Mimi's.

The casket was lowered in silence, and the gravediggers began shoveling earth into the grave. Standing around it were Mary, Sheila, the undertakers, the gravediggers, and myself. In a few minutes it was over. The undertakers stood around waiting to drive us back. Mary waved them away, saying we would walk home. Then, weeping, Mary went to a nearby bench and sat down. I went to Papa's grave and cleaned the dirt from it. Sheila stood a few feet away, watching me. I took a few flowers from Mimi's grave and put them on Papa's.

We began walking the hilly mile back to the house. Sheila looked more beautiful than I'd ever seen her. She had always moved with the grace, ease and elegance of a panther, but now there was a warmth there. When she smiled at me it was almost an embrace. She appeared far more sensual now than she had in her flirting days. I had a great desire to hold her.

As we approached the house, Mary sighed and said, "Oh, Lord, this place sure will be lonely without her."

I told her that my house in Brooklyn would be her home from now on, that she'd be free from all worries.

Mary said, "Thank you kindly, George, but I ain't got no worries. Mimi deeded the house and stocks to me." She began crying again and said, "That Mimi was a good woman! Sometimes bossy an' a little crazy, but one blessed good woman. A saint, by God. Right after they got married, when your daddy got the lung sickness, Mimi traveled with him to Arizona an' the hospital an' then had to sell your big house in New York an' get job as waitress an' then sing in speakeasy to pay expenses for your daddy an' you 'fore she made it big. She never complain or tell anyone or badmouth." Mary wiped her eyes, blew her nose, then pointed at Sheila, "An' there 'nother good woman. I ain't never forgettin' how you come down to comfort Mimi on her birthday; an' I was sick too; an' you took care me and Mimi for a week. No, I ain't forgettin' that." She wiped her eyes on her sleeve and said, "C'mon, let's go in an' have lunch."

The women were about to have lunch. I sat down with them. I thought about everything Mary had said. The women then asked about my flight back to Greece. I told them my plane didn't leave until seven, that I was packed and ready.

Mary said, "I declare, George, you weak an' shakin' an' you say you ain't goin' to eat 'til you get back to Greece an' get — what you call it — your 'lumination — or least not 'til forty days is over."

I nodded.

Mary said, "How you know when the 'lumination come? How you know? How all them saints know?"

I tried to figure out how to answer her. I didn't know. Bishop-Doctor Andrew — as well as the monks on Mount Athos — all had said that when God touched you it was inexpressible. I thought, Is anything expressible? How could I have expressed my misery and helplessness of last April? How can I express my present gladness and peace?

Then, suddenly, I knew it *was* expressible, but not with words. I smiled at Mary, got up, went to her and hugged her. I went to Sheila and hugged her. I returned to my chair. Reaching out, I took an apple from the fruit bowl. I held the apple in my cupped hands, turning it, feeling its texture, looking at its colors, smelling its fragrance.

Silently I asked the apple for permission to eat it; and I knew that permission had been granted. I thanked the apple. I bit into its flesh and began chewing it — feeling its vitality flow throughout my body.

Mary and Sheila watched me and then started their lunch. The three of us ate slowly, without speaking. When we were finished, I telephoned the airline and canceled my flight to Greece.